WIT AND HUMOUR OF HARYANA

RAJBIR DESWAL

BOOKS FOR ALL

(AN IMPRINT OF LOW PRICE PUBLICATIONS)
DELHI-110052

Distributed by
D.K. Publishers Distributors (P) Ltd.
4834/24, Ansari Road, Darya Ganj,
New Delhi-110002
Phones: 51562573, 51562575, 51562578
e-mail: dkpd@del3.vsnl.net.in
visit us at: www.dkpd.com

© **Mrs. Chander Koumudi**
First Published 1991, Edited and Re-published 2005
ISBN 81-7386-271-0

Published by
Books For All
(an imprint of Low Price Publications)
A-6, Nimri Commercial Centre,
Near Ashok Vihar Phase-IV, Delhi-110052
Phone: 27302453
e-mail: lpp@nde.vsnl.net.in
visit us at: www.lppindia.com

Printed at
D K Fine Art Press P Ltd.
Delhi-110052

PRINTED IN INDIA

IN LOVING MEMORY OF
OUR
DEAR DEPARTED
MOTHER

LATE MRS. RAJ ISHWAR DESWAL

HER MESSAGE TO US WAS

*AMOR VINCIT OMNIA**

* Love conquers all

FOREWORD

These are grim days. Any attempt to make one laugh, even momentarily, is welcomed. It is in this context that I feel happy in introducing Rajbir Deswal and his book on wit and humour in Haryana to the readers.

I have followed his writings in newspapers of the region, including the Indian Express and have felt that he knows his land and its people well. His anecdotes and characterisation have the original flavour of Haryana. He sticks to some expressions in the Haryanvi dialect because it is necessary to use it to give the mood and spirit of the people.

Rajbir Deswal claims that such a book is being published for the first time in Haryana. He must be right. In any case, I have not come across a book on the subject. He deserves praise for he has written a book which happens to be a difficult project. It also helps a person to know one aspect of the Haryanvi culture intimately.

Deswal believes that the wit in Haryana is not biting but it does all that 'tomfoolery' is capable of. One may or may not agree with him. One may also feel that the Haryanvi humour is too pedestrian to be made the subject of a book. But these are subjective views. What matters is if you enjoy what you read. If a person has been honest in presenting a true picture of the rural culture and has also succeeded in making others relax and laugh, he has surely done well.

The author admits that one may occasionally feel the jerks of a dialect coupled with an onslaught of Haryanvi temperament while reading the book. One may be tickled by innocent and unoffending but prickly insinuations and may perhaps question the very character of the book for it is a simple narration of routine happenings. But here lies the quality of the work as there is no dilution of the original in the presentation.

The second part of the book introduces certain typical individuals who form an integral part of the Haryanvi society. But for these characters, the life in the rural setting would be dull. These characters are representatives of different traits, commonly found in human beings. I fell the wit and humour of Rajbir Deswal is universal—only the dialect is Haryanvi. It is typical rustic humour that grows from the soil and anybody can enjoy it.

It is creditable on the part of a police officer, and that too in Haryana to be able to devote his time to an academic activity in such a relaxed manner. That he has done his M.A. in English Literature and that he has substantial experience in journalism, perhaps helped him think to such a project; otherwise also, he seems to have a natural talent in narrating the stories of his land.

Prem Kumar
Resident Editor,
Indian Express,
Chandigarh

Chandigarh
September 21, 1991

PREFACE

Why A Book On Haryanvi Humour

Humour in any society or civilization is a reflection of the maturity and vastness which is encompassed in that particular arena. Haryana has undoubtedly been the cradle of Vedic and Aryan Civilizations; a rose-bed of values and virtues cherished by Indian and envied by the world. And here was the need to bring alive to the lovers of culture, a hidden and so far, un-explored treasure of wit and humour, particular to this land with special emphasis on Haryana.

And they say, there is no better a, way to put across your ideas but by way of wit and humour, as also satire. Since the endeavour here has primarily been to make the readers travel along the unstrolled avenues of Haryanvi culture, the approach of the humorist was preferred, lest dullness and fatigue should take the better of the journey.

The First Part of the book contains about fifty episodes which depict one aspect of Haryanvi Culture or the other; this being explained by a small introduction or opening followed by one or two relevant jokes. The jokes are purely original and not much of craft has gone in, so far as their narration is concerned. Everything has been said in lighter-vein and with no malice to any individual or class. All the episodes naturally grow and emanate from the soil, and soul, of Haryana and if one has a nose, sensitive to this fragrance, can enjoy the aroma.

The Second Part enshrines typical characters found in the Haryanvi cultural milieu. One can find these characters in the entire back-drop of Indian society yet here is something unique about them. These Haryanvi characters have been introduced in a manner, as the reader is face to face with them and in turn, they too seem to be coming out of their frame, to shake hands with the readers, humorists and lovers of culture.

Rajbir Deswal

about them. These Harvanvi characters have been introduced ... with them and to ...

CONTENTS

HE-MAN, SHE-WOMAN

The husband-wife relationship in Haryana is quite typical. The reaction of the spouses in different situations can be totally unpredictable. And this tit-for-tat emanates from the situation and not from the hearts, as the Haryanvis have a rosy heart as against a rocky-facade.

Once a wife throwing blandishment, on her husband, requested him to get her a *nath* (an ornament worn in the nose). The husband for some unknown reason was annoyed with the wife, For a little while, he kept silent, suppressing his anger. But the wife insisted, in the most immodest manner, goading her husband that she was not asking for the moon, instead a *nath*. Unable to control himself, he thundered, *"Main tera naak katwaan nai phirun soon ar toon nath kee baat karai sai* (I am all out to have your nose chopped-off and you are talking of a nath) !"

In a situation, quite contrary to the above, the husband was on the death bed. The doctors feared he has lost his memory. They asked him 'strange' questions as to who he was and could he recognise anyone. Sensing the grave condition of her husband, the wife who was standing by the bed side burst out emotionally, *"Don't you recognise even me?"* she asked. *"Yes",* replied the husband. The wife heaved a sigh of relief and said out of love, *"Who am I?"*.

"Why, arn't you my mother!" said the husband.

"Pher to jee liya, mere Sher (You will definitely survive then)!"sobbed the disgusted wife.

NO TRAINING THIS

Well, one who has enjoyed his life, indulging in pleasure, is known as *Khelya-Khaya,* in Haryana. This phrase is also synonymous for easy-go-lucky-types, as well. In this episode let us be with the animals who speak Haryanvi.

The he-buffalo is known for his laziness as the calf of a cow is for swiftness and agility. While the calf can be seen galloping like a horse from one place to another, the he-buffalo is all the time relaxing.

These two were sitting under a tree when the *jhota* (he-buffalo) was disturbed by the *bachhra* (calf). The former asked him to behave by saying *"Bhai itna nahin machya kartey* (dear, have the mind at ease)". The debonair *bachhra* said, *"Kyoon Tau, ji karda ho to aja bhir ley* (uncle dear, here I challenge you for a bout)". The *jhota* said *"alright, what will be the feat like"*. The sportive *bachhra* jumped and said, *"let it be a race"*. *Jhota* who could not even walk with ease replied, *"naa bhai, baithyan-baithyan kaan halan ki haan otda ho to aajya* (no dear, if you want to compete in the art of shaking the ears while sitting only, then come on!)"

Once a mother-crow was teaching her little-one to fly. She taught him well and within a very short time the little one could soar in the sky on his own. Then the mother-crow taught him certain other things like what he should avoid during his interaction with other fellow-birds. She feared an all time danger from the human-beings and this warranted a word of caution against this species too.

"Now be careful and listen to the most important thing," she confided in her little one, *"don't ever trust a human being".* She cautioned the little one that if he saw any body, even gesticulating to him, as if he was having a stone to harm him, he should immediately fly. *"What mother if the human-being already has a stone in his hand?"* asked the little one. The mother-crow declared, *"You don't need any training, toon to khelya-khaya sai, jaa mauj kar".*

PROPER MODE

Despite the claims of development and modernisation, Haryana's heart is still untouched by the so called cultural renaissance. People do not adapt themselves or switch over to newer things but with hesitation, emanating out of innocence.

"Jee master Jee, Jee," is the typical address to a teacher in a village school. Pre-fixing and suffixing *'jee'* adds to the respectability of the teacher. Not strictly going by this notion, at least suffixing *'jee'* is an accepted respectful mode of address in Hindi, if not in Haryanvi dialect.

Once a slightly 'advanced' villager, on knowing the importance of *'Jee'*, directed his *seeri* (partner-servant) to suffix the same while addressing the former. And as said earlier about the Haryanvis' reluctance to adopt "stranger things"; this precluded this *seeri*, of course unconsciously, to include the new suffix in his vocabulary.

While carrying a heavy load of fodder, and panting heavily, one day, he sought his master's help saying, *"tarva dey,"* (help me remove this load). The master looked at him with a stern gaze obviously reminding him of the proper mode of address by saying, *"dhaalh-sar bol"*. And, *"tarva dey, Jee bhee kahai dyungaa* (help me first, and I will add jee too)!" was the obliging outburst.

Making arrangements for the comfort of a guest, another villager knocked at the door of his neighbourer to borrow a cot. The latter replied that he had only two cots and on one he and his father slept and on the other his wife and his mother. At this the villager said that he would arrange the cot from somewhere else but, *"dhaalh-sar sona to seekh lyo* (at least learn how to sleep properly)".

NIHALA THE GUARD

A distantly related uncle of mine had been away, to fight for the British, in Italy, during the second world war. Back-home, he was often addressed as *'angrej'*. There was yet another trio of drunkards who were famous for their jocular nature. One day they asked the *'angrej'*, *"Well, we would all accept you to be an English if you let us know the meaning of thoo* (to)".

The poor 'brown-chaudhry' tittered and said, *"Both of you three come to my place and I will let you know the meaning".* Although I am not aware what did the *'angrej'* tell them but I doubt if even the knowledgeable would tell what is an infinitive, not to talk of a to-infinitive.

Again coming back to the British period, at a manned-railway-crossing was employed Nihala, who would introduce himself as Nihala-Guard, to the know-nothing mortals, out of sheer pride. Once, on a stormy night, completely drenched in rain-water from head to toe, he was there signalling a train, with his english-lantern. Unfortunately, the train rammed in a standing railway engine on the nearby station.

The station-master, who was a Britisher, summoned the defaulter gate-man in his office, to personally explain to him the dereliction in duty. Convinced that he would understand nothing but English, and would feel happy that even the lay-man Indian knew his (stationmaster's) language, he replied,

"Shur in the sharkumshtanshez, when the hawa iz chullunging and the laltun iz boojhanging, what can poor Nihala gaard do (Sir, in the circumstances, when the wind is blowing and the lantern going-off, what can poor Nihala-Guard do)?".

RECOGNITION

When in the town, any act on the part of ruralities, which is not in comformity with the urban way of life, is bound to 'expose' their embalmed identity. Even today, the sons of the soil feel hesitant about their being so 'recognised'. And it is this recognition that is known as *pichhan-jana.*

Once a group of villagers decided to go to Haridwar. There was one among these who was a *hookah-bharania* type (one who does all odd jobs for others). They hired a tonga and knowing his place, our submissive friend sat near the feet of others on the rear of the tonga. At a steep rise, when the tonga was about to roll-back, the driver asked our friend to get down so that he could restore the balance. Got he down, but he would not go without asking the *tonga-wala* as to how did he recognise him that he only was the one who could be asked to get down. The entire group laughed at our friend for he was the one who was *pichhan-gya* (recognised) for his being a *desi*-piece from Haryana.

Now, they decided to have their meals at some good restaurant. As a habit, our friend *hookah-bharania* was late in eating-up his food. The entire group was offered finger-bowls to wash their hands after meals. One of them, seeing the lemon-piece in warm water, squeezed it and drank the lime-water, declaring that it was offered for it was good for digestion. All others followed suit. The bearer, who was observing all this, smiled at our friend, *hookah-bharania,* and whispered the reason, on his asking, in his ears. It was his turn now and he burst into a typically Haryanvi Hostel-type laughter and said, *"Thum saarey bhee pichhan-gye",* (you too have been recognised).

I would not hide from the readers when I was also once 'recognised' in the metro-politan city, Delhi, when I was working there as a Sub-editor in a Weekly. I offered the fair to the auto-rickshaw driver who said, *"Thank you, Chaudhry Sahib".* I was stunned for I was also *'pichhan-gya'.* And I swear, I was attired tolerably smart, and truely, I spoke nothing while in the auto-rickshaw, but still......!

INCORRIGIBLE

Although, the english-people's claim of possessing the quality to laugh at one's own self and at one's own cost, is universally acknowledged and appreciated. But we too have, in Haryana, a class of characters, who would rather feel proud, of being publically called fools. This class is known as *'bhayaya'* types in this region.

To elaborate, *bhayaya* is a thick-skinned person, having his own rationale to justify his every unusual and abnormal deed. Such behaviour, if commented upon, critically, leaves the *bhayaya* no more wiser; instead he feels exhilarated and lifting-out-of-himself and describes the criticism as an 'exciting commentary' on his (ab)normal behaviour.

Once an above-said type was wearing a *safa* with a long *tuhra* (long end of the turban left on the waist to reach the hips). This is a symbol of one's social acclaim; hence, the longer the *tuhra*, the more is the person recognised and almost adored.

Now, some one who knew the shady character of this imposter pointed out to him that his *tuhra* was very long. Replied the man that it was not a *tuhra* but the growth of *maror* (vanity widely known in Haryana as superiority complex). And further he said, figuratively, that the *tuhra* was a *maror ka dahlah* (branch). The one who had raised a point said laughing that such *maror ka dahlah* could lead any body into trouble and that people usually beat-up, such a man with wetted-*juti* (a wetted shoe hits hard). Replied the shameless *bhayaya*, with a grunt, and rolling the eye-balls on one side, straightening one or two of the errant strands of the *tuhra*, *"Beaten-up I was, and not on one occasion, but the maror ka dalha kept growing like this only"*.

Once an old-*bhayaya* in a street, looked up only to find a naughty young girl, about to throw dirt below. *"Aey chhori, dull ja"*, (stop there, young girl). The girl held back the dirt and threw voluptuous smile asking, why shouldn't she throw the dirt and went on to say that would he prefer cold water instead. *"No, No"*, cried the *bhayaya* below. And with an inviting type gleam in her eyes, the mischievious girl teased in a soft tone this time, *"Should I myself fall down!"* *"Bhakaawai- sai...!"* (You are making a fool of me, aren't you?". Poor *bhayaya* could hardly suspend his disbelief and the young girl did really have him there.

NO BROTHER OF MINE

Not only in Haryana, but in the entire region a *galaria* is the son, who accompanies her mother to her new husband's place on re-marriage, done as a result of previous marriage broken; death, desertion, divorce, elopement, for any of these reasons.

Once a *galaria's* brother, born of his new father disputed his (*galaria's*) claims to the ancestral property in a Court of Law. The proceedings were on with the judge asking the plaintiff, his name.

"My name is Dhapoo, huzoor," replied he.

"What is your age?", the judge asked.

"I am a couple of years younger to my sister Dhapa," he said.

"When was Dhapa born?", the judge questioned out of disgust.

"It was in the same year, huzoor, when my bapu had sown makki in peepal-ala khet", was the irritating answer.

Enough was enough, the judge removed his spectacles and questioned further as to on what grounds did Dhapoo dispute the claims of his brother.

"He is not my brotherm, he is a galaria huzoor", Dhapoo argued.

"Now, who is this galaria," the judge said with genuine discomfiture and asked the counsel to explain who was himself not aware of the argued 'nomenclature'. Distressed, the judge asked Dhapoo to explain as to who was *"this Galaria"*.

With folded hands Dhapoo prayed:

"God-forbid if your father dies huzoor......" . Dhapoo was checked by the 'standing' counsel to mind his language, but the benevolent judge realizing Dhapoo's innocence as also the ruggedness of his dialect, observed that it was in the interest of justice, to allow the plaintiff, to explicitly clarify his contention.

Dhapoo spoke and spoke he till he brought home his point, for fear of interruption, his terse being, *"God-forbid, if your father dies maai-baap, and my father marries your widowed mother, and you accompany her to our house as a galaria, will you become my brother? Will you have any right over my land?"*

ODDS AND ENDS

Once a *dever* was getting married. He invited his *bhabi* to join the ladies' sangeet. She refused on the pretext that her finger was hurt and she could not sing. The *dever* questioned the relevance of the injury to singing, *"Why, shall not I need to put my finger on the lips while singing"*, she replied. It is customary in Haryana to cover the lips with hands or cloth while singing, so that the identity of the individual in a chorus is not revealed.

The other day, the same *bhabi* approached her *dever*, to milk her cow. The *dever* would not oblige and took an excuse saying that he had a swollen mouth. *"But you employ only your hands for milking the cow and not your mouth"*, the *bhabi* argued. *"Why, shall not I produce the sound of puch-puch, kich-kich, by rounding my lips, if the cow goes out of control"*, replied the naughty *dever*.

On another occasion, a busy-*bhau* handed-over her small child to her old father-in-law and went to the fields. The child started crying and the old man took it out for a ride. He reached the bus-stop where he was advised to give a little tea to the child for it would be hungry. The old man had the tea prepared but it was too hot and the child did not stop crying. Another fellow, sitting nearby advised he old man to pour some tea in a plate and give it to the child. To this, the old man replied that the child could not drink and could suckle only. Still another fellow chastised the old man thus; *"Yeh moochh kis din kaam aaweingee, chah main dubo kai balak nai chusa de,* (what use you will put your long moustache to, why not dip them in the tea and allow the child to suckle at them)".

BIMARI AUR PHAYDA

In Haryana's countryside, the best medicine readily available for an injury is used mobil-oil; and for any emergency case a mixture of *doodh aur haldi, ghee aur geru*. However, these cause a nauseating sensation, hence the fondness for recipes for a little 'non-serious sufferers'.

Someone had a stomach-pain and the well-wishers prescribed different 'panaceas' for the ailment. The patient however did not respond to accepting any of the bitter medicines. Someone at a distance advised that he should be given some *halwa* to eat. Convulsing a little more, the patient shouted, *"Can't you all listen to the prescription of the one standing at the doorstep".*

Two Haryanvis had gone to some religious congregation where *halwa* was being cooked in big cauldrons. Steam was coming out in the form of bubbles making a sound of *phus-phus*. One said, *'dekh, halwa saskai sai* (see how the hatwa is sobbing)". *"How do you feel like?"* the other one asked. *"As if I should jump into it"*, replied the former.

There are joint families in Haryana where out of many members, one normally remains a forced bachelor through out his life and is called *be-aulada* (issue-less). Well, one fellow of this category had to take care about his meals etc. himself.

While other brothers' wives served their respective husbands with good food, this man was neglected. He procured some *bura* for taking with his meals; he would take out a little *bura* and eat it. When others objected to this "special arrangement" of the poor fellow, the misdemeanour argued in humble tone, *"you must all be thinking that I eat bura just out of my fondness for sweets, the case is otherwise; actually it does me phayda (good)"*. *"Why! are you pregnant?"* retorted one of his brothers. Well, a pregnant woman is made to eat a little more nutritious diet.

HARYANA STANDARD TIME

Much is meant than mentioned, when we talk of "Indian Time". And for Haryanvis, *bakhat* (time) is an expression not only of hours and minutes but certain situations as well.

There are certain phrases like: *bakhat parna* (distress); *bakhat ana* (death); *mara bakhat* (misfortune); *bakhat bicharna* (a calculative move); *bakhat ka marya* (weather-beaten); *bakhat ka paji* (one who misses an opportunity) and so on. And those in the Bangar belt will say, you wait, I am coming within *duodh-mint* (one and a half minutes). Hands tattooed with designs of watch, is a common sight.

A watch in the dowry is a major item, the bride-groom being illiterate notwithstanding. Well, one fellow had a field through which the road passed. He stopped a bus once, only to ask the time from the driver by showing him his watch.

And once early in the morning, two farmers were quarrelling over diverting the water channel because it was the other's turn now. The first one said, *"You see the watch and if you don't know how to see the time, at least wait for the cock's crowing; at least the latter can't be wrong"*. Battered the second. *"It is my field that needs watering and not of the cock!"*.

I was then preparing for my master's degree examination, in the peaceful atmosphere of my village. I asked the servant to wake me up at 4 O'clock in the morning and the poor fellow could not rise himself. I immediately ordered his 'sack' only to receive his old mother at our door. She had perhaps come to know about her son's 'dereliction in duty'. She pleaded, *"Beta, spare him this time, in future, he will wake you up not only at four, but even earlier than that, be it six or eight."*

A Lubricated Kick-Back

The daughter-in-law and mother-in-law relationship is as ignominious in Haryana as it is every where in the world. Both characters are infamous for their 'committed' contemptuous explosions towards each other. Admittedly, the daughter-in-law is most of the times at the receiving-end.

Once, a daughter-in-law was in a very ugly habit of denouncing her mother-in-law publically for the latters cruel behaviour. She would often complain to the neighbouring ladies about her taunts, torture and crookery of this sort or that.

Well, in the villages, they ease themselves in the open preferably when it is dark, be it early morning or late evening. This vituperative daughter-in-law rose very early one fine wintry-morning and left for the open space to ease her. It was dark all-around. She sat near a bush and observed that some other 'lady' was also sitting there. Actually, it was an old-punk who had wrapped himself in a blanket due to cold. Now, the lady began her tale of woe and routine cursing of her mother-in-law. And as women are not supposed to talk to any senior male member of the village, the old man out of his 'modesty' did not answer to console the lady.

"You know, this time my saas did not provide me sufficient ghee, knowing fully well that I am pregnant," the lady continued to complain. She further asked the one who was sitting by her side, *"Why don't you speak?* Enough was enough for the old man who shouted, *"Main key teri khatir ghee key bare bhar rahya hoon* (Do you think, I have containers full of ghee for you)". Rest can be imagined!

JUST-MARRIED

Thanks to the precious-little social awakening that marriages are not decided in wombs these days in Haryana. But the practice of child marriage still continues, in some communities, as also in some areas.

A boy and a girl were getting married and while the priest was busy chanting *mantras*, a dispute arose between the would-be husband-wife over a small creature. The girl said, *"Bhai, kiri* (Brother, it is a small ant)". The boy rebutted, *"Bebe, makora* (Sister, it is a big ant)".

Another, just married teenager, was very fond of mares. And there was a mare-keeper also. He was approached by the former requesting to spare a mare. The mare-keeper suggested the boy that he was now married and had a *bahu* (bride). *"Bahu to toonye lele, main to ghori lyoonga* (you have the bride and give me a mare)"*, replied the 'He-teenager.'

A tender-aged shepherdess was married to a matriculate spouse. He told her that he would take her to the town for honey-moon. Without understanding, the girl accompanied him and enjoyed their marital bliss for about a week. When the boy suggested to return, the girl reminded him of the promised honey-moon. The boy told her that the time spent by them in isolation was honey-moon itself. *"Oh! was it? But I have spent such a time with the fellow shepherds in the fields many a time,"* the 'innocent' girl replied with a grin.

Some parents are always eager to marry their children just to get rid of the responsibilities, domestic and social.

Once a father, who had a son, who had by then, only entered his teens, was insisted upon by his father to get married. The boy protested and said that he had not come of age. But the old man would not relent and got the son married.

On the night of consummation, in an apparent bid to make love with his 'healthy-spouse' he tried to go near her and the newly-wed bride jumped either this side of the bed or the other. The inhibited poor girls in Haryana do not make advances and also do not respond to advances by the husband as 'taught' to them by the *sahelis* (friends).

Now our He-man, exasperated, called his 'experienced' father by shouting. *"O-babu, now come and atleast help me catch this Bua* (father's sister) *of mine."* In Haryanvi dialect this reference is not taken for its literal meaning.

CAUGHT ON THE WRONG FOOT

In the otherwise taboo-ridden and convention-conscious society of Haryana, there does exist a class of slackers, who would look for an *"upaay"* (a convenient method) to get by the intricacies of the rituals, in matters religious.

The ashes of the dead are consigned in Ganga at *Har-kee-Pauri* (Haridwar). It is commonly believed that such a ritual will help the departed soul have mukti (salvation) and this practice is an obligation on the part of the kith and kin of the deceased. The person who takes the ashes to Haridwar normally is tempted to see a few other mythological places like *Lakshman Jhoola, Bhemgoda* etc.

Once a non-serious type took such ashes and in an anxiety to return home hurriedly, he consigned them into the *Yamuna* instead of *Ganga*, the latter being farther away. Back in the village, he was asked by others if he had rightly performed the ritual, and the guilty-conscious fellow emphatically asserted that he did. *"Did you see Bheemgoda also"*, one asked. In Haryanvi, *Goda* is a knee. The defaulter said trying to become actually realistic, *"Ram! Ram! It was such a gorgious goda, I had never seen one in my life."* Then some one asked if he had seen *Lakshman Jhoola* as well; *Jhoola* is commonly known as a swing. *"Oh, yes! while swinging I could feel the Ganga itself sometimes rising and sometimes falling. The villagers could easily see through the mischief.*

On another occasion, a youngman, who was all-in-all in the family, was getting married, quite a worldly-wise fellow, he did all the jobs himself and did not trust anyone. He knew about the greedy priest also that he would ask *sawa-rupya,* everytime he performed the same ritual. The ceremony began and the *purohit* while chanting hymns wove a red, sacred thread around a mud-pebble declaring that it was Lord Ganesh. He demanded *sawa-rupya* for Him. The bride-groom quietly hid the symbolic lord in his hands. The *purohit,* after chanting a few more hymns demanded another *sawa-rupya* for Lord Ganesh and started searching for Him. The embarrassed priest looked here and there and finally towards the bride-groom who told him that Ganesh was not as greedy as the *purohit* was. He said, *"Lord Ganesha's share was only sawa-rupya, and after taking it He has vanished, now what next?"*

THE UNCONTROLLABLE CORPSE

Mudlana village in Sonepat District is known all over the region for its inhabitants' jocular and humorous nature. This humour of course, sometimes is very wild and rustic and results in ugly happenings, many times. The village-urchins, in particular are said to be 'naughty beyond repair'.

Once heavy floods deluged the whole village including about a 2 kilometers stretch of Panipat- Rohtak road. The road was badly damaged and for the convenience of the drivers, the authorities put long bamboo-*lathis* with red flags, where water was very deep and vehicles could be 'held up'.

Much to the inconvenience of the villagers, the buses did not stop to lift them the whole day. The urchins came to their rescue and during the night hours removed the red flags and fixed them on the 'declared safe passage' with the result that the morning saw a big line of standard vehicles and passengers with their pants, trousers and *dhotis,* up, crossing the *'Mudlana channel',* with their foot wear in hands and other belongings on their heads and shoulders.

Mudlanaites were in for a shock the other day, when a passerby (let us call him a *musafir*) was going on foot to the other village, nearby. An octogenarian had died and the villagers were going to the funeral ground carrying his *'Arthi',* in a revelling mood; villagers bid a happy farewell to a person who dies attaining and spending a considerably long and contented life.

One of the funeral party member shouted at the *musafir* of ours, telling him to beware as the *murda* (dead) might *farak* (react offensively); quietly the man passed-by.

After a couple of days, this *musafir* met the same party, on his way back, when some young person had died and the *Arthi* was being carried in an atmosphere of gloom. Now was the turn of our *musafir* who shouted at the party, *"Is it the same uncontrolable farka hoya murda, who you are carrying for the last three days, or it is somebody else!"*.

WHAT ABOUT YOUR CUSTOM?

A variegated and not a composite cultural is confined within the contours of Haryana. Certain areas are geographically known e.g. *Bagar, Bangar, Khadar, Nardak and Mewat,* for reason of soil, resources, weather conditions and population etc...And no doubt, there are cultural divisions also, based on the above said factors. But as a whole, the social interaction between these areas has given birth to certain customs, traditions and conventions which put together are called *rivaaj,* which differ from one area to the other. In this region, if one enjoys a feast at somebody's place, it is called *jimna* unlike Uttar Pradesh where *dawat* is more commonly used.

Once a mother-in-law asked her daughter-in-law to lay the *khaat* (bed or cot) for the latter's father-in-law who was to relax after returning from the *jimna;* obviously, one does full justice to the feast on such occasions and returns 'over stuffed'. The daughter-in-law wanted to know the purpose of laying the bed. To this, the mother-in-law replied that they had a *rivaaj* to relax after the *jimna,* hence the need for laying the bed. And curious to know the *rivaaj* prevalent in the area to which the daughter-in-law belonged, the mother-in-law put a question to know that. Replied the daughter-in-law, *"Maaji in our area, the cot is carried along for jimna".*

SEEING TO BELIEVE

About a couple of decades back, people in the rural setting did not know or seek to know the things around them. They largely confined themselves to the affairs of either their own village or at the most of their *guhand* (a cluster of villages). There are several *khaps* (clans of the same origin or gotra); in Haryana, *Ghatwala* being a prominent one. Now they are more commonly known as Maliks and are famous for their fraternity.

The chief of this *Gathwala Khap,* at one time, not very long ago, was Chaudhry Ghasi Ram, popularly known as *'Dada Ghasi'* for people held him in high esteem even beyond the khap-land. Dada Ghasi had died before the death of Pt. Jawahar Lal Nehru. And when Pandit Nehru died in 1964, somebody broke the news to an innocent villager; the latter replied, *"Dada Ghasi har bargey nahin rahe, is pandit ki key hasti thee?* (The likes of Dada Ghasi are no more, how could this Pandit match their statuses?)"*. No doubt Mr. Nehru remained almost on the top of Indian political scene for more than half a century.

One busy evening, another villager heard on the transistor that a man (Niel Armstrong) was to land on the moon. He went to his fields for watering the crops and returned in the morning as if he was cheated. Removing the spade from his shoulder he remarked in utter desperation, *"These radio-walas do not tell any truth about the weather; all the more they forecast unimaginable things I kept looking at the moon throughout the night and I saw nobody walking (landing) on the moon ?"*

AFTER ME THE DELUGE

Invitation to any happy occasion is called *nyota,* in Haryana and the village *naai* is usually entrusted with this job. The old punks feel ignored if they are not invited to 'grace' any such occasion. Normally, one or more members from a *kudhi* (a joint family unit) suiting the convenience of the host, are invited through the *naai*.

Once an orphan girl was being married away by her three, young brothers. The poor chaps forgot to invite a fussy old man, just the next door. Now this man laid his cot in the middle of the street and puffing at his *hookah* he started cursing and criticising the arrangements, much to the embarrassment of the 'should have been hosts', for the old man.

This man would now pass humiliating comments on the *baratis;* he would not permit any vehicles to be parked in the street and he would disapprove of the *baratis* being fed on the roof-tops. Sensing the trouble, the three brothers discussed and enquired if the old man was sent *nyota* or not and realizing the mistake, they immediately sent the *naai* to invite the old man.

"That's like good boys", the old man remarked and ordered the removal of the cot and his *hookah*. When he was welcomed by the three brothers, he greeted them for 'excellent' arrangements and declared that the *baratis* were fed on the roof-tops only; and where else? And, except the streets, where else could the vehicles be parked? Finally, he said that, *"The*

boys would after all be boys only but they have ultimately behaved in a responsible manner". The old man later personally extended his courtesy to the *baratis* and supervised the marriage affairs himself.

Another old man was very fond of joining marriage parties. A *barat* was soon to leave for another village. But this man had not been invited by then. He was getting impatient and when he couldn't help, he called the member-in-charge of the *barat*. He asked him about the number of *baratis* as also who were the persons invited to join the *barat*. The in-charge of *barat* informed the old man about the number and also the names of the persons who were sent invitations. Sensing the old man's desire, he said, *"And Tau, you too should be joining"*. *"That's all! That should be all! After all why should you be inviting an army of men for a barat"*, said the old man.

HIS NEPHEW'S UNCLE

Despite the best efforts off the constitution-makers, caste considerations could not be washed off our psyche. Every individual belonging to which ever caste tries to maintain the supremacy of his caste over that of the other. Haryanvi society being no exception to this.

The *Naai* is known for his clever moves and the Rajput for feeling proud of his chivalry. Once two representatives of these two strata of society detrained on a lonely village Railway Station. The Rajput was carrying his bag and the *Naai* accompanied him to their common destination, a village nearby.

To break the ice, as a *Naai* always has a tendency to know thing and make people know them; he asked the Rajput, *"kaun log?"* (what caste are you?). As if the latter was awaiting such a query, he replied, *"Rajput—Raja-Ka-poot"* (Rajput— a king's son) and having established the 'royal connection' he handed over the bag to the *Naai* to carry it.

The *Naai* thought it was too embarrassing for him to be a carrier; however, he walked silently. The Rajput giving an upward twist to his moustache then asked the *Naai* his caste. Ready as the *Naai* was, quickly he retorted, *"Naai ar Raja-Ka-Bhai ar tera chacha* (I am a Naai and a brother of the king and thus your uncle)". And very cleverly he handed over the bag to the Rajput thereby putting him to unexpected embarrassment.

BY THE SAME LOGIC

Haryanvis are, most of the time, carried away by illogical things; and at the same time they can be equally rational by being illogical in their assertions.

A story is prevalent when a Member of Parliament, well-known for his having been physically thrown out of the House many a time brought home a point to the innocent audience, while speaking at an election meeting. The 'point' being that the water the farmers were getting for irrigation was useless as *'bijli'* had already been taken out of it. He was obviously referring to hydro-power generation.

So, four idlers were sitting and to kill time, one of them suggested, *"O.K. can any body tell the names of four towns ending with pat, immediately". "well, one is Panipat"* said one, *"and the other is Sonepat,"* said the other. Third one's imagination crossed the *Yamuna* and the answer put forth was, Baghpat. Now the forth one, having been left out with no answer quipped, *"Kharkhoda". "No, No, No, it does not end with pat, no!"* cried the others. Pat came the reply: *Our Dhanpat (a common name in Haryana) is married in Kharkhoda, so I am correct".* And all the three accepted the assertion gracefully.

QUOTING STATISTICS

There is said to be a sharp contrast between the *Jats* of U.P. and those of Haryana. While the former are known for their shrewdness the latter are a little innocent. There is a saying also in Haryana that *"U.P. ka Jat aur pathar ka baat; jitni bar toley ghat-e-ghat"* (A Jat from U.P. is like a stone-measure which reduces every time it is weighed). Since Yamuna is the only dividing line of the culture and contours of the two states, the social interaction on both sides is fairly common to both.

Once a Jat from Haryana went to some landlord of his caste in U.P. On having enquired about the hospitality-formalities, the Jat from U.P. asked his Haryanvi counterpart about the crops he produced and his total gains. The poor man replied that he harvested about a hundred quintals of wheat and about 20 quintals of gram and told that a couple of acres of standing sugar-cane was the *"Ramji's daya"* (Almighty's grace).

Having had two-three puffs at the *hookah* the Jat from Haryana asked the Jat from U.P. about his gains. *"Some one-thousand quintals of wheat; five hundred quintals of gram and about fifty acres of standing sugar-cane"*, was the impressive statistics quoted. To this the man from Haryana retorted, of course after five-six puffs of *hookah, "You are right chaudhry, I only was a fool, to have replied first; otherwise you were not going to weigh my gains carrying takhri- baats (scales) to my village"*.

ONLY IN SMALL MEASURES

People in this region are not very fastidious by nature. If you just ask them *"chaai-pani"* or address them as "Chaudhry Sahib, Rao Sahib, Lalaji, Thakur Sahib, Sardar Ji, Shah Ji, and so on, they are easily won-over.

Even the females can be easily pleased if you take them around for a mela or atleast promise such an 'outing'. While having tea or any drink, a villager can easily be identified for the *'chusarkee'*—sound made by inhaling air through mouth from rounded-lips, while drinking. These people are so unaware about their surroundings or exhibitionism; they have a tendency to stick to fundamentalism on the contrary.

It is a common saying that one would give a *bheli of gur* (about 5 kg) and refuse one stem of sugar-cane; so uncalculative people, one would like to be with! If some one wears neatly washed dress, the others might cut jokes on his having become an *'angrez'* or a *'shaukeen'*, or someone may ask, *"Going somewhere? Aren't you?"* In cities, one finds people of very old age going for cinema but in the villages, even if the youngsters venture for it, they are objects of public criticism and ridicule. There is a famous satirical *raagni* which suggests similar feelings *"Saath saal ka boodha bi dekai phillum solman saal dekhiyo key hoga"* (What will happen if a man of sixty, sees the movie Sweet-Sixteen).

I remember my father telling me that my great grand-father would bring one *"thaan"* (full roll of cloth) and every body in the family would wear clothes from the same common *thaan*. So simple people they would never crave for variety or choice.

Once a house-wife took her husband's lunch consisting bread, *lassi* and onions to the fields where he was working. When a couple of loaves were left, as the big onion was consumed, the man enquired from his wife if there was any more *gantha* (onion). And stretching her pupils towards one end of the eye and looking at her husband, asked, the lady gave a quizzical smile calling him *"Chatorey....aren't you one"*. Well, *chatora* is a person who is fond of variety of delicious things.

THE DELHI-RETURNED

People not only in this area, but in South India as well, have a craze to see Delhi, for the reason that the place has not only been a seat of power since centuries, but is associated with innumerable historical events attached to *"Dilli"* for being that of *"dil walon kee"*. Hence, one would naturally feel inspired to venture a trip to *Parantha wali gali* in Chandni Chowk, and why not a Chaudhry from Haryana, for that matter.

Well, he reached Delhi, and the first thing the people of this region do after reaching some place is, eating. This man was quite impressed with the meals he took. Having spent a few hours at the *Kutub Ki laat and Lalkila,* he returned to his native village.

The 'Delhi-returned' Chaudhry lost no time in collecting a crowd of curious *'gaamris'*—as he called the villagers, after his arrival back. *"Well, these dilli-walas are very hospitable",* he declared in the assembly around a *hookah, "You know all of them, those in a hotel, danced attendance on me like any thing. A couple of boys greeted me outside and escorted me to a tipaai* (table) *inside. The other one came and cleaned the tipaai and another followed him with a bakhora* (glass) *of water. Still another came and asked about whatever food I liked to have. And you know, all of them insisted me to have more and more like we do when we feed the baratis".*

"But didn't you have to pay for it", interrupted one. *"Well that's right, you will naturally have to pay, but the most fascinating thing was that they were all bateus* (sons-in-law) *wearing pagris. Don't you think it was respectful to offer maan* (money given as a token of respect and recognition) *to the serving bateus after having food at their hands".* In Haryanvi dialect *bateu* means not only a son-in-law but a guest too.

BANGRU BOLA

A major part of Jind District with the adjoining semi-arid type zones, constitutes what is popularly called Bangar. Although men and women of this area are said to be very beautiful and there is a *raagni* much prevalent these days, *"Aey Chhori Bangar Ki teri kamar maili hori sai"* (O, girl from Bangar, your waist—and untidy!).

The modern cultural renaissance has not at all touched this chunk of land which lies almost in the heart of Haryana, and for this reason people of this pocket are recognised as the most innocent. And again for this very reason the so called educated ones, out of their sheer pride and shrewdness call them *'bolas'* meaning simpletons or fools.

Once a snake appeared in some village shop-keeper's shop, who jumped out of his *guddi* and raised an alarm. Our friend bangru happened to pass-by. On sensing the shop-keeper's shaken-self, he took a *lathi* and entered the shop to kill the snake. Now the shop-keeper bolted the shop from outside. People gathered there and asked him the reason and the shop-keeper replied, *"Both are good for nothing; at least one would be finished".*

Another Bangru had not seen a bus although he had seen the train, once in his life. When one fine morning, a marriage was to be solemnized and people were waiting for *barat*, the bus carrying the *baratis* was seen approaching the village fast. The Bangru was terror-stricken and ran towards the village warning everybody of the danger approaching, and at the same time telling everybody to hide themselves in the nearest available safe places as the *"Rail ka Kaatru"* (bus) had gone amock and astray. Well, *Katru* is the calf, when separated from its mother-cow runs helter and skelter. Bangru thought the bus was the young-one of a train.

WHAT HARYANA EXPORTS

I had been to Bombay during the winters once. I was aware of the climate there but leaving nothing to chance, for I am quite prone to catching cold, I took along a pull-over. My host in Bombay, caught a glimpse of the pull-over in my suit-case and laughed at me saying *"You will not need it here".*

I just smiled at him but after a little while I doubted if he would provide me a quilt in the night. And I asked my Haryanvi host about it. *"We don't keep quilts as we don't need them here",* he said, *"but we have one rajaai (quilt) only to be used in an S.O.S. condition".*

I was curious to know the relevance of a quilt to an S.O.S. condition and perhaps reading the expression on my face, he said, *"Relax, it is only to humble-down the shivering if anyone in the family is attacked by Malaria"*.

Before paying us a visit in India, a relative of mine in U.S.A. telephoned his brother (also in America) if he needed anything from India. *"Not from India but from Haryana"*, said the brother and demanded, *Rohtak ki Revri and Panipat ka Panchranga Achar, "ek mooshtyan-ka-pinjra (a mouse-trap) bhi lete ana"*. He said. I wonder if the Westerners have started recognising India, no longer a country of snake-charmers, but of mouse-trappers.

A DATE WITH HARYANA 'RUDE-WAYS'

I pity the Video Coach travellers, who really miss the opportunity to laugh with convulsing stomachs and aching jaws, by not travelling in buses where Haryanvis keep the atmosphere very lively and entertaining by their bold but apt remarks and sharp wit out of their buoyancy of spirits. Singing *ragnis,* cutting jokes at each other, making allusions, comparing situations, they make the *'ghur-ghur '* of the vehicle float above the mind.

Most of the bus drivers and conductors, whose behaviour is often dubbed as 'unscrupulous, uncouth and rustic' by the fussy modernites, make the atmosphere inside the vehicle lively by their comments, emanating from the occasion itself and really they do not hurt the simple and innocent folk, as they speak the often described *lath-maar* dilect of Haryana which easily percolates their (passengers') open-hearts.

The driver would comment on a lazy boarder *"should the bajewalas* (band) or *geetan-aali* (females singing a chorus) be called for your *aarti* (welcome)?"* And no less naughty would be the conductor who will retort if a 'mutilated' currency note is returned to him saying, *"iskee key aankh dookhni aah ree sain* (are its eyes soring)?"* And every body inside would enjoy, the juxtaposition of the driver and imagery of his 'colleague-of-conduct'.

Once some body reserved his seat by spreading his handkerchief on the seat which was occupied by an old man wearing a big turban. The former came and tried to convince the old man that his seat was already reserved "by spreading the handkerchief". Unmoved, the old man replied, *"Well, if I spread my whole length of turban on all the seats, will they be mine?"* Weighty argument, wasn't it!

Another Chaudhary with his big tobacco-affected brown moustache silenced a bob-cut, Jeans-junction-blonde, who claimed reservation by telling the man that, *"Yeh seat hum logon kee hai:"* And pat came the reply, *"if you claim to be a log (meaning a man, in Haryanvi), are we fools who are carrying this heavy load of moustache on our face for the last half-a-century?"*

Drivers are equally naughty and their reflexes work to the extent that they are able to judge the 'latent traffic sense' even amongst the travellers. Very often you would find a hoard of ladies seeing-off their *Sakhi* singing *"Sathan chaal pari ey mere dab-dab bhar aye nain"* (Our friend since childhood, is leaving for her in-laws and I am about to break-down at the thought of her departure)".

Now, the driver watches all this drama: the bride hugging each lady and every body 'consoling' her. But the driver has to pick-up his next 'time', so he puts the vehicle in the gear and with the sound of the accelerator, he sees the bride jumping anxiously to board the bus. Then in the 'infamous mirror', he watches the couple settled down and chatting and exchanging glances, through the transparent veil, of the hither-to-fore hesitant bride.

Sometimes the comments on the physical description of co-passengers are very apt. I was once travelling in a Chandigarh-bound bus and behind me was a well-built 'Haryana-gentle-man' (honestly in the sense you call a Sikh-gentle-man). I heard some comments of dispute. A freak-voiced fellow was heard asking this Haryanvi friend of ours to give him way, to which the latter 'gave a pass' in a coarse and thundering voice *"likar-jaa"*. How do you talk? "the former complained and received an even more offending remark, *"I will give you one and your head will bang against the bheent, (wall) Susra, Bakra-sa!."*

This was enough for me to look back and what I saw was a lean, spectacled, V-shaped, cheeky young man standing there with a Confucious-type growth of beard on his aptly commented face.

A young conductor asked the age of a suckling baby from his (baby's) young and beautiful veiled mother. The lady sensed the conductor's mischievious intentions and sat un-moved. Jilted, the conductor asked the age of the baby again and the reply he received from the now un-veiled lady was, *"Bahatar saal* (Seventy-Two years)".

HUMBAI JUMBLE

'Humbai' is a typical Haryanvi word meaning, yes. This word is very commonly spoken in Rohtak, Sonepat Districts and adjoining areas in the Suba (Rural Delhi).

Once a representative of these areas was button-holed by a foreigner near Qutub-Minar. The foreigner, who carried with him a Hindi-English dictionary questioned this gentle-man about the veracity of the fact that two upper stories of Qutub Minar were pulled-down after a plane-crash. *"Humbai"*, he received the affirmative answer but couldn't follow it.

Concluding that it was a Hindi word, he scanned through his dictionary but couldn't find the word. Curious as he was, he put his problem about the confusing word to another gentleman who replied that those who were illiterate said *"Humbai"* and those educated said *'Hann-ji'*. *"Are you educated?"* asked the foreigner, *"Humbai"*, said unconsciously, our friend *Dilli-sube-ala*.

NAUGHTY OLD BOY

'Chhora' is another word in Haryanavi dialect which has different meanings in different contexts but basically it means a boy. The connotations it carries range from

youthfulness; smartness; bravery; to mischief and modesty.

'*Kaacha Chhora*' means a boy of very tender age; '*Chhora Paar Ka*' means a man with buoyant spirits from an alien land; '*Chhora (Caste) Ka*' means a page-boy; '*Chhora Parya sai*' means an old man looking young; '*Chhori ka Chhora*' means a nephew from sister's side; *Chhora Shyam* means a handsome person (Shyam was Dada Lakhmi's favourite actor-singer, disciple), and so on.

As we paint our faces and dye our hair in an urban atmosphere, these artificial charms are discarded in the countryside for fear of being pointed-out. Old ladies would often chastise their husbands who try to grow hair or dress-up smartly saying *"rahan dey, Chhora na banai"*, in the same sense an old English lady calls her paramour of equal age, *"you, naughty old boy!"*.

VARIETY—JUST RELEASED

Habitations in Haryana are known by various names. Cities and towns are called *shahars* and *kasabas* and their sub-division are called *mohalla, gali and patti* etc...Similarly, villages are also called by different names in different areas. In Sirsa, Hisar and Bhiwani districts, small helmets are called *chak or dhani;* in Karnal, Kurukshetra and Ambala, they are called *dera;* in Rohtak and Sonepat villages these have two or three divisions namely *pana;* in Jind, the villages are divided into *kudhi* (small joint family unit).

In the foot-hills of Shivalik near Kalka, Pinjore, Naraingarh, Sadhora etc. ten families make a *takra* and eleven *takras* make a panchayat. In Assandh, Safidon, Kaithal, Guhla, Pehowa and other areas adjoining Punjab, the villages are called *pind*. In Haryanvi, pind is also the name of a recipe made by mashing the *paranthas* with ghee and *bura* which becomes a semi-solid sweet paste. Normally, the Haryanavis carry the *pind* with them while travelling and it is considered to be a sort of 'packed food'.

Once a Jat and a Sikh were travelling by the train and were sitting face to face with each other. The Jat felt hungry and took-out his *pind*, turned his back and started eating. It is customary in Haryana to eat with turning your back against the non-eaters. Since there was none else in the compartment, the Sikh wanted to break the ice and initiate conversation, he asked his co-traveller about the name of his village, saying, *"Tera kehra pind hai?"*

The Jat confused this *'pind'* with his recipe and without understanding the question fully, he passed-on a part of the *pind* to the Sikh, who accepted it and ate it. The query having remained unanswered, he asked the Jat again, *"Tera kehra pind hai?"* The Jat did not want to part with the remaining *pind*, so he did not oblige the Sikh neither by offering nor by answering. When the Sikh asked him the third time, the Jat lost patience and said, *"Bajre ka hai, Bajre ka! (It is of millet, man, millet!)"* And having finished it, he asked the Sikh about his *pind.* The Sikh replied that it was Lalroo. Bewildered, he commented: Quite unheard; but it must be some latest variety of food-grain.

AREN'T YOU A MARD

In Haryana *"Mard"* has two meanings. One has connotations relating to ones sexual potency or Hemanship and the other means a husband.

And moustache are, of course, a symbol of somebody's *mardangi* (virility). Once a tall and hefty fellow was driving a bi-cycle down the slope where happened to be the village well. A lady with her *doghar* (two pitchers kept on the head, one above the other) was also there. This lady, while crossing over to the other side, met with an accident with the speeding-down, cyclist, resulting in making her *doghar* fall and drenching her completely from head to toe. *"Can't you see, don't you have eyes, couldn't you stop your cycle, you moochhan aley"* cried the lady at the 'fallen' cyclist. *"But, are the moustache brakes poor lady?"* remarked he.

On another occasion, a thief broke into the house where a couple was sleeping. The husband and the wife noticed the thief breaking in, but did not move apparently out of fear. Now the wife whispered in the ears of the husband, *"listen, are you listening, there is some body in the house"*. Although keeping vigil, the husband lay unmoved. Again his wife coaxed him, of course by whispering. And the husband questioned as to why should he only challenge the thief and invite trouble. *"Well, you are a mard"* the lady chastised. *"That's right in your case, but I am not the mard of the chor,"*. The he-man husband submitted very calmly.

NOT SO STRANGE BED-FELLOWS

The *guru-chela* (master-disciple) relationship in Haryana has never assumed much of significance for the reason that mostly this duo consists of wandering *modas* (ascetics). It is primarily for acquiring the assets owned by the *gurus* in their *ashrams* that the so-called disciples have been found to be most of the times the cronies of their 'spiritual masters', at some stage of their life, or the other.

So, the non-serious type of *guru* and *chela* were readying for sleep on a winter night, in their hut. The *guru* asked his *chela* to shut the window as the cold breeze was becoming intolerable for the half-clad *guru*. *"Guru ji cover yourself with the quilt and for you atleast the window is closed,"* said the lazy *chela*. *"O.K. put off that diya (earthen lamp) bacha,"* asked the *guru*. *"Guru ji cover your face and all will be dark around you,"* suggested the un-obliging *chela*. Quite annoyed, the guru commanded, *"Acha bacha shut the door lest some one should break in"*. And with a banter, the *chela* quipped, *"Look guru ji I have performed two tasks; the third one, you carry out yourself."*

Another of the above described cult of *chelas* was setting forth for Haridwar and the hut of a *sadhu* (hermit) was on the way. He stopped there, and just by the way, asked the sadhu if he needed anything from *Har-Ki-Pauri*. *"Get me a good shankh (conch) bacha,"* the sadhu demanded.

The villager returned from the pilgrimage and on reaching the village-outskirts, he was reminded of the sadhu's demand. He searched for, and laid hands on a dried-up, donkey-skull. On reaching the *sadhu's* hut he found him sitting crosslegged on the *assan* (platform) out side the *kutia*.

With an expression of pride in his eyes, he offered the sadhu the 'sought gift'. The sadhu tried in vain to produce a counch-like sound by blowing breath through the skull. Ultimately, he said, *"But it does not produce any sound bacha."* Replied our friend the pilgrim, *"It is only a matter of time baba ji, otherwise its sound could be heard at miles' distance."*

NOT BY COURTESY ALONE

Barter and Cooperative systems are not new to the people of Haryana. Articles are exchanged mutually, to fulfil the common, limited needs of, and, amongst the ruralites. But this exchange definitely involves the art of borrowing; and if otherwise, refusing with a smile, instead of a breath-blocking 'NO-P'. I think people of Haryana are neither good at borrowing nor lending, partly because of innocence and partly because of the dialect.

Once some body went to borrow a bull, for ploughing, from his neighbourer. The former had, at some occasion, made some unpalatable remarks against his neighbourer who took it to heart and kept the fire of revenge burning within him. This man refused to oblige the borrower, saying that his bull could not be spared.

Disappointed, the borrower walked away till he was beckoned by his neighbourer, immediately, to be told that even if the bull could be spared, he would not have lent it to him atleast. Another, apparently a wise man, sitting with the neighbourer, asked him why did he call the borrower again, after refusing once very plainly. The reply was: *Nyoon bina iska bhitrla nahin dookhta* (his inner-self could not be hurt otherwise).

The latest version of this episode is that some body went to borrow a horse from another villager, who refused the former saying that the horse had been sold away and was not there in the stable. In the meanwhile, the horse sneezed loudly and hearing it, the borrower said that the horse was very much there. *"If you believe an animal and not the man, how foolish would it be to oblige you"*, was the argument put forward.

There is a saying much prevalent in Haryana, *"gaadi-kai kaatru-bandhna"*, which means that if you do not want to lend your car, say that your pet-dog is tethered to it.

Beggars are not choosers, but in Haryana it is otherwise. A Haryanvi beggar would not flatten his face or twist his tongue or spread his palm, or make his eyes sink, or bow with a bowl before you; instead, with bulging eyes and swollen cheeks he would importune, *"Ghaallai sai ak chaaloon"* (Do you offer or I should make a move)?

AND DID I REALLY GO!

House-holders usually welcome the guests in the countryside in Haryana also keeping in with Indian culture where a guest is likened to God Himself. Attendance is danced in the actual sense of the word on every 'dropper' for that matter. And there were times, not very long ago, when guests were entertained for length of time, even beyond weeks and months. This hospitality has undergone a drastic change, for the worse, these days; but what to do if the guest is like our friend Tapku Ram.

Once Tapku Ram stayed with his relatives in some village for over one month. The poor hosts, an issue-less couple, could not enjoy their 'privacy' for the presence of the familiar and 'shameless' relative, Tapku Ram. The couple often discussed their problem with the neighbourers who consoled them saying: *Dane dane pai likha, khane wale ka naam.* The lady of the house, however, said that it seemed to her that Tapku Ram's name was written on their wheat-bag.

The couple thought of a clever plan to ease-out the guest who they considered no more worth looking-after. An agreement was reached between the two that they would enact a mock-fight and the husband would beat-up the wife and she would cry. And seeing the disturbed atmosphere in the house Tapku Ram will himself decide to leave the place.

(Act I. Scene 1st)

Husband   (*Shouting at his wife*) You have been spending whatever I earn. After all money is not grown in the fields.

Wife   What should I do if your relatives create problems in our family. Should they not realize that....(*sobs*)!

Husband   Shut-up! You.....(*slaps*).

Wife   (*Sobs*) All right, I am going to my *peehar* (father's place). Bring garlands for your relatives (*sobs*) and make them sit on your head.

Husband   I will.....! (*slaps again*)

Wife   (*Crying*) O.K. it is well in time that you have opened my eyes. (*sobs*) I am leaving............

    (*Exit Wife and enter Tapku Ram*)

Tapku Ram What happened? I think I am the root-cause of the whole trouble. I too am going.

    (*Exit Tapku Ram*)

    (Scene 2nd)

    Enter Husband and wife:

Husband   (*To the wife, embracing her*)

    So, he has left, but did I really hurt you?

Wife   (*Smiling*). And did I really cry?

    (*Enter Tapku Ram*)

Tapku Ram And did I really go?

    (*Curtain falls*)

RESPACTABLE POCKET-MONEY

Once an enterprising farmer of Haryana opted and went ahead with his plans to run a poultry farm. The poor man, 'educated' by the agriculture experts and convinced about the idea of practising a side-business besides cultivation of land, hurriedly established a small unit of poultry.

One day, somebody posing himself to be a 'taxing officer' visited the poultry farm and seeing the health of the birds enquired from our farmer friend as to what feed was offered to the *'mote-taze murge'*.

Thrilled at the admiration of his birds, the poor entrepreneur said, *"Kaju-Kishmish sarkaar"*. *"And that is why there are irregularities in your accounts"*, thundered the tax-officer, boomeranging the reply on the farmer. The latter offered him his 'tax' and felt spared.

The next day, a health officer came and put the same question to the farmer. Now the bird-keeper was reminded of the 'tax' he had to pay for his statement about *Kaju and Kishmish*, so pleaded he with innocence, *"Babu ji, the birds go-around and eat any sort of rubbish they find worth consuming"*. *"So, that is the reason behind so many cases of indigestion and bad stomachs being reported and that too after consumption of infected-meat"*, he scolded the farmer. The poor man was taxed again.

Now it was the turn of the police officer. On being fascinated to see the healthy birds, he also 'interrogated' as to what was being fed to the birds. The experienced, twice-taxed farmer thought of a calculated answer to get by, saying, *"Huzoor, I only give a ten-paisa coin to every bird as day's pocket-money and honestly I don't know what do they eat".* Thus having been disarmed, the police officer raised a legal point, *"So, you leave the birds free for awara-gardi; all right, send a dozen healthy murgas with 'respectable pocket money' to my residence.*

CARRY-ON DARLING!

It is an accepted fact that women work more than their male counterparts in Haryana whether it be domestic jobs, agriculture chores, bearing children, looking after in-laws, taking food for the (once in a while), ploughing husband, fetching water etc. etc.

And all the more cumbersome it is to work in 'veiled conditions'. On the other-hand, the husband enjoys most of the joy-time either at *hookah, chaupar,* cards, conversation, attending marriages, visiting the *shehar* many times, listening to *raagnis* and all that can be counted as variety and entertainment in the Haryanvi cultural milieu. Snubbing the wife for any work left undone is also his pride-prerogative; the urban-husbands may envy this man from Haryana.

Spending weeks and months in the *sasural* (in-laws place) was until recently a common practice for the holidaying-husband. He would eat and drink and sleep and enjoy the hospitality in the *sasural* for many days altogether.

Someone went to his *sasural* and who so ever enquired about him in the *dahleej* (lounge), this man was introduced as *"Murti ke ghar-ala* (Murti's husband)". This man for his long stay and repeated introduction, unconsciously cultivated an auto-suggestion for himself and as a result nearly forgot his name and remembered only the introductory appellation, that being-*Murti ke ghar-ala.*

Back home in his village, he was asleep in his father's *dahleej*. When the father returned home after sometime, he asked him, *"Who is there?"* Now the man, obsessed with the 'introduction' replied from under the cover of his *chaddar, "Murti ke ghar-ala* (It is I-Murti's husband)". The furious father gave him a *laathi* blow and chased him to the fields to work where his wife Murti had already been working since morning.

Having produced a number of children, another such husband left his wife only to remain busy with the work of looking after his progeny throughout the day. Returning from a *hookah*-session, he cried at his wife, *"What are you doing Bhaagwaan?"* And the answer echoed against his ear-drums: *"Tere Karmaan nain rowoon hoon* (I am suffering the punishment for what you have done)!" *"Carry-on, Carry-on, you are busy with my work only!"* the shameless husband replied.

JUST BORN GENERAL

The Haryanvis are proud of their progeny and they can not tolerate any comment against their 'physical features', atleast. Also, the Haryanvis feel ashamed at producing *weaklings*.

The recruiting officer while selecting soldiers in a Haryana village rest-house was shouting at the top of his voice at the same time cursing the new generation for their 'chiken-chests', 'Pigmy-size' and 'frail structure' obviously, there were no 'healthy-men' available for recruitment.

Ruldhu, an old man was passing by when he over-heard his 'boys' being so commented upon. He went near the recruiting officer and bared his hairy chest and said in a challenging tone, *"Well, if you find fault with the chest of our boys, come, measure this and select me"*. He pointed towards his expanded chest. The officer yelled, disgusted of course, *"We recruit only jawans in the Army, get lost you old punk."* *"In that case why can't you recruit me a Jarnail* (general)", quipped Ruldhu, with a haughty smile.

RESERVED TREAT

Beating up wives, in Haryana is not very uncommon. And the unfair-sex in their bid to thrust their male-ego, very frequently indulge in thrashing their spouses, for trifles, and at the slightest provocation.

It is so happened in a mela that the poor wife incurred the wrath of her husband by disobeying his command of returning home. This man would not let any opportunity go when he would beat-up his wife, so frequently as 'at the drop of his *pugri*'.

He started roughing-up the poor lady in the mela itself when a huge number of spectators watched the *heroic-deed* of this man.

Somebody intervened after a little while and said *"Now stop this, such acts are not done in a mela."* *"Theek sai, gharaan ja kai nayari pitoonga* (All right, I reserve a treat for her when we return home)", said the fisticuff-happy man.

STRICTLY PERSONAL

When it comes to telling a doctor your disease, the Haryanvi females fight shy of the situation and would use phraseology of their own. For example, if you feel a sinking heart, you tell the doctor, *"as if there is a fan-on, inside the body"*. And as not many doctors would understand all this, they check and cross-check by repeating questions by way of which they can diagnose the malady.

A doctor from an urban background was examining a village lady who had some gynaecological problem. When it comes to referring to sexual intercourse, the Haryanvi females use the word *'baat-cheet'*, and in Hindi this word means conversation, too.

Well, the lady began, *"When my husband does baat-cheet with me, bleeding occurs."* Apparently disturbed, the doctor fixed his gaze on the legs of the stool, the lady was sitting on, and questioned in disbelief, *"Now that I am doing baat-cheet with you, do you feel the same problem?"*.

In a T.B. Hospital the doctor was examining the patients. An attendant sat on a stool outside the doctor's room. This attendant would caution the incoming patients and gesticulating at them would ask them to cover their nose and mouth with some cloth, so that the T.B. germs in the patients' breath did not affect the rest, including the doctor.

A village woman came and tried to gain entry into the doctor's room not heeding the caution. The attendant held her back and asked her to cover her mouth. The woman brushed him aside and reached the doctor. The doctor too, on finding a (T.B.) patient so near, without a covered mouth told her to obey the attendant's advice, first.

"Naheen aati manai baans (My nose is not affected by your foul-smelling hospital)," told the lady and sat near the doctor for examination. Obviously, she had thought that because of the commonly stinking clinics, everybody was cautioning her.

WEREN'T YOU ALIVE THEN?

Although the joint family system is fast breaking in Haryana, with equal pace in the countryside all over India, yet there are family units living in perfect harmony and where the members have regard and recognition due to them, and the duties assigned to every member are carried out, 'meticulously'.

In a family, usually there are some earning members; some drones; and some are really poor simpletons, good-for-nothing. Well, a bachelor of the last category was asked by his elder brother to fetch his (brother's) wife from her parent's village. In Haryana, *devars* usually fetch their *bhabhis* if the elder, busy-brother, has no time to spare for this job. This *devar,* knew nothing about the formalities of conversation to be observed and being unmindful of pleasantries to be exchanged, he was briefed by his elder brother to simply answer the questions and enquiries in *"yes or No",* so that the poor fellow could over-come his 'modesty'.

Having reached the *bhabhi's* village, he was asked about *raaji-khushi* (well-being) of his elder brother. He, after applying his mind, replied saying, *"No"*. Shocked, the hosts asked him if his brother had died; and the tutored idiot said, *"Yes"*.

What followed can be well imagined and in the din of cries and clamours, he requested the *bhabhi's* father to send her daughter along. The 'bereaved' father told him that his *bhabhi* could not be sent as she had become widow, her husband having been 'informed' dead. Convinced, our friend, the *devar* returned to his village and on his way-back, his elder brother button-holed him in the fields itself and enquired as to why did he come all alone and without the latter's *bhabhi*.

Out of sheer innocence, the younger brother declared, *"Bhabhi to vidhwa ho-gee"* (Bhabhi has become a widow)". The elder brother snubbed him saying that how could it be possible till he was alive. *"Weren't you alive"*, replied our 'enlightened' friend, *"when Bua (father's sister) became widow just a couple of years back"*, and he moved ahead, still sad.

WORKING RELATIONS

Relations are well defined in Haryana's rural cultural milieu. For example, there is a saying that:

> *Gandey tai gandiri aachhi,*
> *Gur tai meetha lahla,*
> *Bhai tai bhatija pyara,*
> *Sab tai pyara sala.*

(A piece of sugar-cane tastes sweeter than the whole stem; And sweeter still is viscous than gur; A nephew is more lovable than a brother; And the most lovable is the brother-in-law).

But the 'addresses' which define these relations, if used in a different context mean entirely different things. If you want to tease a person call him *Mama;* if you have to yield to someone, call him *Foofa;* if you have to get rid of someone call him *Khasam;* and calling somebody *Susra* or *Sala* only indicates your casual annoyance with the addressee.

An old lady complained to her young, but innocent nephew, as to why did he beat the *bahu,* his wife. Pleaded the man, sitting with his knees reaching his temples before the old lady, *"Budhiya, suppose you are my wife, and you don't obey me, shall I not beat you up?"*

Well, *"Kaka"* in this region has different meanings. In Punjabi it means a small boy, but in Haryanvi it either means an uncle or a father. On Delhi-Ferozepur Railway route, Narwana and Jakhal towns are the representatives of Haryanvi and Punjabi dialects, respectively.

A father and his son were travelling in the train and on reaching Narwana a co-traveller asked their relationship with each other. *"Well,"* replied the father, *"He was my kaka* (son) *beyond Jakhal but here onwards, I am his kaka* (father).

A youngman was walking through the fields and behind him, in perfect Haryanvi tradition, was his newly wedded wife. There was a small *rajbaha* (water channel) and the man jumped on the other side while the lady could not. The veiled lady asked the youngman, her husband, for help. But the 'chivalrous' husband demanded, *"call me kaka first".*

DOWN TO EARTH

So far avenging insult is concerned, Haryanvis have a typical characteristic to retort, or strike without waiting for the iron to be hot; failures notwithstanding. Not at all crafty, they would not make schemes and plots, which requires time, planning and patience, rather the earlier the insult is avenged the better it is, no matter what should be the occasion, or the manner.

An old villager visited his friend's son in the town who had secured a good job for himself. He requested the officer to use his good offices and get the former's son employed. The officer tried in all earnestness by contacting so many persons on telephone in the presence of his deceased father's friend, the old man.

And finally, he told him that he (the officer) could not do anything on such a short notice and that he would let the old man know 'his position' when he would be visiting the village on weekend. But the old man was not convinced and thought that the boy (officer) had given him a slip.

Back in the village, and fully convinced about the officer's intentions of not getting the needful done, he waited for the latter's arrival. Well, this old man had a *laanda jhota* (a tail-less He-buffalo). And when the officer came to his village on the scheduled weekend, he met the old man with his *laanda-jhota* on the way.

Immediately, the old man held in his hand the remaining 6 or 7 inches long tail of the animal as if it was the receiver of a telephone, and stood resting against the back of the animal, shouting, *"Hailoo; Bhola Ram from Heaven? I am Molar Ram speaking from the Earth, I want to tell you that your son has become such a big officer that he will now make us aware about his poujeesun (position)...yes, he is the same kodhi (a leper) who played in our arms but it is for your information that he has really become a badda-aadmi (big-man)".*

The busy old man on the 'celestial line' was interrupted by the officer only to be told that a job had been arranged for the former's son.

MOUTH-FULS AND GLASS-FULS

People in Haryana are exceptionally fond of *desi ghee* and milk. In their usual conversation also they can not forget praising certain other eatables for their delicious taste as well. In the semi-arid zones of Haryana, *bajra or makki* (millet or maize) is the only grain which is available for making bread. And the wheat floor is considered to be a thing of luxury.

Once two representatives of these areas were talking when one declared that the, *"aaloo ki dal ar gehoon ki roti"* were really delicious and tasteful to eat. The other gave quizzical looks and asked as to if he himself had been lucky enough to taste such food. *"No,"* replied the former, *"it was at Rohtak and I had only seen a constable eating the same".*

Two villagers were praising the qualities of *desi ghee* and the good it could do to human body. One said that *desi ghee* was something which could be mixed with anything and that 'mixture' could be eaten with added taste. Another, apparently an incorrigible-type, over-heard and quipped, "can you eat tamakhoo (tobacco) if *desi ghee* is added to it?" No comments!

One meaning of *chhori* in Haryanvi dialect is the daughter the other, a girl. Once a *naai* had gone with *sidha* (gifts including eatables) for a girl, married in a distant village. On reaching the village, he was offered milk, as it is customary in Haryana, but to the annoyance of the *naai* who was very fond of milk, the glass was very small and would not contain as much milk as would satisfy him. Immediately after taking the glass in his hands, the *naai* looked at it and said, (apparently to suggest the girl) *"Perhaps the manufacturer could not make a still smaller size of glass but my worry ends with the Bhaagwan chhori atleast, who would definitely offer me a couple of such more glass-fuls of milk".*

OH, CHHOREY BOBBY

Till some years ago, movies were known as *Jinda-danas*, in Haryana; *khel; Sanima and Phillum* being the current callings. Some of the movies e.g. *Nagin, Raja aur Rank, Sholey* etc. have been very popular with the Haryanvis, if we see the record of the last four decades only. Without knowing the music-director Hemant Kumar, most of the *raagnis* are still sung on the tunes of *Nagin*, particularly the *Been-Lehra* of *"Tan dole, mera man dole"*, etc. And no less contribution was made to provide the *taraz* (tune) for *raagnis* by *"phirkhi wali"* of *Raja aur Runk* fame.

But the best known and seen movie with the Haryanvis, as else where in the country also, has been, Bobby, perhaps. The cumulative effect of the craze can be gauged from the fact that it was not the question with these cine-goers whether they had seen Bobby or not, but as to how many times they had seen the movie.

During the Bobby days if the youngsters visited the town, on seeing the college girls they would remark, *"Oh chhorey-Bobby"*. The husband would promise their wives not a mela but, Bobby. Not to talk of these, the town-migrated son would assure his mother he would show her Bobby, when she visited him in the town, breaking away with all inhibitions and reservations of the prevalent parent-children relationship in Haryana.

And my village was one step ahead of all, when they all named the ugliest of the women as Bobby, just out of mischief. And I remember, she had tried to drown herself in the nearby canal, but was rescued by those only who had bestowed the 'title' to the poor lady.

During those days of Bobby-craze, after seeing Devdas, I came out of the cinema hall only to find a *"cheated chaudhry"* who said in a loud voice, in the Devdas-hang-over affected crowd, *"Was it a film? My money spent on Bobby bought me the best bargain when the girl bites the boy's ears, eloping with him on the phit-phit!"*

On another occassion, a *phillum-fan* and father of a newly born son was snubbed by his old mother by telling *"if you will continue your obsession with films like this, you will be ruined and will not be able to feed your son"*. *"Well mother"*, replied the son of Haryana, *"my son feeds on his mother's milk as yet, it can be only your son who will remain unfed"*.

OPPORTUNITIES UNAVAILED

Haryanvis do not repent at their losses. *'Al-leh!'* only is the expression at the biggest loss, and that is all. Of course, they would recall the missed chance in the most humorous and witty manner.

In a *barat,* a father and his son had, had their stomach stuffed with sweets upto the throat. Those who were serving *ladoos* and *jalebies* had nearly exhausted their containers. During the last round, the father accepted one more *jalebi* while the son refused. Next morning, back in their villages the son recollected the feast as if still having a taste in his mouth and told his father, *"Babu, jai main wa jalebi dhara leta, to bus dharai leta* (Had I accepted that jalebi I had really had it)".

Having played cards till mid-night, a group of hostelers decided to sleep. Appreciably, a member of the defeated group kept turning sides and could not sleep, till he knocked at the door of his partner at 3 O'clock in the night. The latter invited him inside and our restless player complained, at the same time puffing out the smoke of his *biri, "Jai toon woh ikk na gerta to hum jitey paray they* (Had you not thrown that ace, surely we could have won)".

Lord Shiva and his consort *Parwati* were said to be travelling through some fields where they spotted a dumb *Jat.* The kind hearted *Parwati* prayed to the Lord to restore the *Jat* his speech. Shiva informed *Parwati* that it would be 'risky' to do so at that juncture. But *Parwati* prevailed upon him. The blessed *Jat* on being bestowed speech said, *"O' Mode, isi suthri lugai kit tai mari* (Oh! a hermit and a beautiful woman—how come)!" The divine wrath left the poor *Jat* bereft of his voice again. And the *Jat* although could not speak now, but had the expression of *'Al-leh'* on his face.

GOLDIE-OLDIE

Although there are exceptions but the oldies in Haryana are not that fussy. They are self-contained people, and would feel relieved after handing over all property rights to their male heirs immediately when old age dawns upon them. Perhaps this is the reason for their being lively and jocular but at the same time they are rational as also aware about their surroundings.

Once a plumpish stranger was walking through the village and on realizing that the lane might be a dead-end alley, he confirmed from an old lady sitting on her *pidha* outside her house, *"Likar jyanga* (shall I pass-through)"? *"I don't know about you, but an elephant, I remember, had passed through this street parkai* (last year)," "replied the old lady", obviously commenting on the person's bulky constitution.

It so happened in a village *chaupal* that some matrimonial alliance was being proposed by a few guests and at the same time opposed by an old punk for some unknown reasons. The oldie would not have his way until he had convinced the guests about the bad reputation of his village. So, he shouted at the playing children, *"Balko, kyon Jehaj kai dale maro so, yoh gaam to pahalyanye bahot badnamm sai* (children, why are you pelting stones at the flying-plane, this village is already notorious for its bad reputation)". And this had the desired effect; the alliance was decided broken.

Often the oldies in Haryana are left with the job of either weaving ropes, or for *rukhal* (guarding fields against stray animals), etc. Once a newly wedded daughter-in-law took the day's meal for her old father-in-law in the fields. The food consisted of some bread, onion and pickle. Back home in the evening, the old man declared that the house would be ruined by the spend-thrift *bahu* very soon, for she had taken two vegetables in his food. While he had his food with only one vegetable. Obviously, he was referring to onion and pickle.

Asking for *aag* (fire) for the *chillum,* from any house, is very common for *hookah*-smokers in Haryana. Once an old man with a "youthful heart" developed fancy for a young bride in his neighbour-hood. In the absence of male members, he would enter the house by asking an old lady in the house, if *aag* was available; and this woman would permit him inside.

This went on for a few days till the bride left for her parent's village. Unaware, the man entered the house and asked the old woman about the availability of *aag* in the usual manner. And the old lady, who by now had sensed his intentions replied from behind the veil, *"aaj to aag paanch aali motor tai chali gayee* (Today' *aag'* left for her parent's village, by the bus, at five, in the morning)".

NAUKRI KE LATKE

There is a saying in Haryana *'haanji ki naukri-naanji ka ghar',* suggesting without any doubt that your being a yes-man guarantees smoothness in your job, otherwise your place is in your home and not in office.

Well, to secure a job, you have to be through the mill of an *interview*. This word is quite known even to the illiterate parents in the countryside for they have to 'arrange things' for their candidate-child's *Jindgi,* figuratively used for *naukri* (job).

An interview for some post was in progress and there was obviously a crowd of candidates keen and curious to know as to what was being asked by the board members. Every candidate after the interview was surrounded and almost heckled by scores of other candidates trying to fish-out what could be, their probable question.

And Lo! a blank-face sneaked from the door and was immediately button-holed. He disclosed that the board showed him a map and asked him to pin-point "Delhi". One fellow realizing the difficulty of locating a place in the map lost no time in seeing a map in a nearby office and ensured where Delhi was.

This man was asked by the board to pin-point the river Ganga, which he could not. Confused, the man replied out of frustration: *"Do you all intend to drown yourself in the Ganga",* and pointing towards Delhi he asked *"why don't you ask about Delhi which is here, exactly here".*

Another interview was being conducted at a District Headquarters for a petty post in co-operative department. The question put forward was as to which was the capital of India. Pat, came the reply, *"Roitakh"* (Rohtak). All the members raised their eyes towards the candidate only to listen, *"Had I said Delhi, would you have selected me?".*

A youngman, seemingly a candidate, at another interview was seen very impatient and keen to be interviewed by forcing his entry inside. The board members felt offended and asked him to enter when his turn was announced. The man kept his cool and told the board to select somebody else by saying, *"Main to batahan aya hoon ke mere bharose naa rahiyo jee"*. (I have come to tell you all that kindly don't keep waiting for me).

A DREAM COME TRUE

Shouldn't be Haryana, with a sizeable population, be proud of producing atleast three eminent sportsmen, namely, Chandgi Ram, Sat Pal, Chand Ram! And at one time even Kapil Dev, was called the "Haryana-lad".

Definitely, in Sports, the spirit weighs more than the self, hence no regrets for Haryana for they are high-spirited people. And particularly when Ben Jonson appeared in my dream the other day and revealed that he had been to Haryana once, only to take an important cue; his hard-luck, notwithstanding.

I asked him as to who advised him to visit us. He replied that it was John Lever who took eight wickets with the help of Vaseline while playing Cricket in India, once. Well, on Johnson's insistence, I narrated a personal college life experience to him; the dream continuing. The college tournaments were being held in front of our hostel. Bhima, a wrestler came running to us and asked if anybody had *"Sanad-ka-ghee"* (guaranteed pure *ghee*). *Sanadh* means a certificate.

Anyway, one of my hostel-mates offered him the desired' booster. "Bhima took a little of it and rubbed it on his nose. He left the hostel only to return knocked down before the count of three. He caught hold of the boy who had supplied him the booster-dose," accusing that it was not *sanandh-*

ka-ghee (guaranteed) and hence his failure. The boy was however rescued.

"Thet ees saffesent (that is sufficient)", interrupted the collosus-figured Ben Johnson. He shook hands with me and left.

On waking-up I felt pain in my palm, had tea, and switched on the television. My God! there was Ben Johnson on the T.V. screen with a Gold Medal. It can well be imagined as to from where did Ben Johnson have the idea to take steroids— apparently this was a cue from Bhima's booster-dose i.e. *sanandh ka ghee*.

BEHIND THE PERIOD

Idg for is, *haj* for has, *same* for shame and *phool* for fool are some of the very common examples of Haryanvis', pronunciation of English words. But their understanding of English too, most of times carries signals as if the language was 'derived' from Haryanvi dialect.

Really, I am true, care for a few examples? 'Hooda' is a sir-name in Haryana and the other acronym "HUDA" stands for Haryana Urban Development Authority. The pronunciation of both being the same. An executive engineer of H.U.D.A. introduced himself to another Haryanvi officer, as "I am XEN, H.U.D.A." and, *"Baitho Hooda Sahib"*, was the receiving noble gesture.

Well, in the University (that too the one in Rohtak) my friend Himmat Singh was contesting for University Presidentship. A dispute arose which was settled with the opponent, who was seemingly a sober cityite. And while parting, the latter shook hands with Himmat Singh, smiled at him and said, *"see you, tomorrow"*.

Himmat Singh's anger knew no bounds and he blasted, *"kaal Kay dekhaiga, aaj dekh ley, teri...."*. The man had literally translated 'See you tomorrow' in the local dialect.

Once an Inspector of schools in a remote village-school entered the class-room, wrote, 'NATURE' on the black-board and asked the class to answer what it was. The class-room echoed with one voice, *"Naatoorey"*. Red with rage, the Inspector gave a stern gaze to the teacher and asked him to demote the entire class by one standard. *"Well sir, this will be done, but will it not effect the student's phatoorey* (future)", the poor teacher replied.

And the best is yet to come. A lecturer told a naughty student, *"Meet me behind the period, when I am empty"*. Poor fellow was well retorted, *"Why sir? Has my father opened your buffalo"?*

IN WESTERN COMPANY

As said earlier any foreigner with white skin is known as *angrej* in Haryana. A representative of this species once came across a Haryanvi woman. As he was hungry, he asked for food from her, gesticulating; making his hand reach his mouth. The Lady got the point and by putting some *saag* (vegetable) on the *roti* (bread), she offered the meals to the *angrej*. Well, eat he did, but only the *saag*, and returned the *roti* saying, *"Thank you, please take your plate"*.

A Haryanvi had gone to America and back home he was relating his experiences to one of his friends. The conversation was like this:

"You know they have a free society, we don't have it like that in our Haryana".

"How?"

"I said hello to a lady and she smiled, we don't have it like that in our Haryana".

"Then?"

"I extended my hand and she held it, we don't it like that in our Haryana".

"Then?"

"We walked hand in hands and she took me to her house, we don't have it like that in our Haryana".

"Then?"

"We went inside her bedroom and she bolted the door from inside, we don't have it like that in our Haryana".

"Then! Then!"

"Suddenly her husband came and we had to open the door".

"What happened then?"

"It happened exactly like that what we have it in our Haryana".

S.H.O., MY FOOT!

It is a common saying that the Police-*walas* are not good either for friendship or enmity. There was a time, when even after the British had left the country, a constable's presence in a village was something to be afraid and suspicious of. The only happy lot were the *'pulis ke pithoo'* (touts).

Once a small-time *chakkiwala* happened to visit a police station where the S.H.O. was interrogating suspects in his own and widely known 'method'. The sight was unbearable for the poor *chakkiwala*. The S.H.O. turned towards him and shouted, *"You lala, I had asked you to send me a bori (bag) of wheat and still, I find you standing there, agape. Should I.....?"*

The poor man promised, and on his return related the entire incident to his younger brother who did not approve of the 'promise' and decided to talk to the S.H.O. himself.

He reached the police station and witnessed the same 'interrogation'. He closed his eyes and put fingers in his ears as he could not bear the sound produced by the *sachputtar.* Now the S.H.O. turned towards the 'energetic and bold' brother of the *chakkiwala* and asked him the purpose of his visit.

"Huzoor, I had come to ask if the wheat had to be sent ground or otherwise," replied the latter.

"Is your mother sitting here to grind the wheat," cried the S.H.O. The poor man promised the needful and returned with one more job assigned.

On another occasion an innocent complainant reached the police station eating a guava. He was intercepted by the Sentry on the gate, who hit him with his rifle-butt, for entering the police station *"while eating the amrood"*.

The poor fellow was received by a Havildar inside and after hearing what had transpired between the Sentry and the entrant, he also treated him with a slap. He was produced before the S.H.O. who also kicked him and ordered him to get out.

The same treatment was meted out to him while he was coming out of the police station, in descending order, till he fell down. He murmured to himself, *"Wah rai pulis alyo, thari pakar bhi buri ar chhod oos tai bhi buri* (Kudos to you O' police-*walas*; your apprehension and release are equally torturous)!"

SHEETAL JAL

A South-Indian scholar had come to Kurukshetra. He approched a *ricksha*-puller and asked him if he could take him to the *'Vishvavidyala'* thinking that if he said 'University'— an English word, the illiterate fellow would not understand.

The non-plussed *ricksha-wala* asked from others if they knew the place where *Babu ji* was to be transported. None seemed to know where the *'Vishvavidyalya'* was. Some one suggested, since the man wore scholarly looks, he must be interested in going to the University. Convinced, the *ricksha*-puller asked the scholar if he wanted to go to *'Unabishti'*.

"Yes, amko University jana ay jee", the Scholar said.

"Babu ji aap bhi hum anpadhon ke saamne angreji kaat-a-tey hain, (Why do you talk in English with illiterate like us)", the poor fellow complained.

Once a *barat* was being served in a village. The Haryanvis serve the marriage party themselves and the services of bearers are not requisitioned. Some one is entrusted the job of serving the *puries*, the other serves *saag*, still other sweets, curd water etc.etc.

The fellow who was offering water was a Shastri ji, who spoke chaste Hindi. While pouring water, he said *"sheetal jal, sheetal jal."*

Back in the *chaupal*, the *baratis* usually comment on the food served. One of the *baratis* complained thus:

"You know the fellow who was offering that sheetal jal, mara bata kora paani pyagya (the scoundrel made me drink nothing else but plain water)".

THE LIKE OF HITLER

Immediately after attainment of freedom, a group of Haryanvis had gone to see the Republic Day celebrations at Rajpath in Delhi. They wanted to have a glimpse of Jawahar Lal Nehru. Many loud-speakers were blaring.

The function was over and the gathering began to disperse. One of the group members was still anxious. He asked his friends if they were able to see Nehru. *"Yes"*, they replied and enquired of the poor simpleton if he could also catch a glimpse of Nehru. *"No"*, said the cheated fellow, *"This bhompo (loud-speaker) kept on telling that Nehru had come and I kept looking in it but Nehru, I suppose, kept hiding in it and did not come out."*

Some years before that, when Indians were fighting for the British in the alien lands, two ladies were talking about a naughty character in the village. The conversation was like this:

"Anh-ree, Ramphall is not seen these days in the village".

'*Don't you know that he has joined the Fauj (Army).*

"Oh! I see, but one thing now I am sure about".

"What?"

"That the village, the country and the world will be devastated now completely!"

"Why so?"

"Do you know that Hitler is a big anari (a greenhorn) and our Ramphall is no less!" A rare comparison indeed!

Wit & Humour of Haryana

Part-2

COPING WITH *BARATIS*

It is only on rare occasions that people in Haryana's rural setting dress themselves up and revel with ecstasy and exuberance. Getting ready to join a *barat* (marriage party) begins days before the actual time to fetch the bride comes around. The *barati* starts accumulating dress material, borrowing from friends and relatives. He arranges a white *dhoti*, a dazzling coloured *kurta*, a stuffy *pugri*, and even a pair of *jutis*, much in advance.

In Haryana any handsome and well-built male is often referred to as having been a born *barati*, as beauty and smartness add to an otherwise rough and tough fellow.

While in the bride's village, the *barati* has a different way of talking and walking, so it is common to refer to a man who walks with pride as having the gait of a *barati*.

Having reached the bride's village, the *barati* selects and reserves a cot for himself in the *chaupal*, where arrangements are made for the entire *barat* to stay. Some of these *baratis* break-up into groups and play cards, smoke *hookah*, or take another bath, using as much soap and oil as they can, showing no mercy, what so ever, for the bride's poor father.

The comparatively younger crop among the *baratis* prefers to roam and loaf in the streets of the bride's village. Since they are recognised as guests of the entire village, their petty mischiefs and remarks are overlooked by the villagers.

Dark glasses (mostly green or blue), with brand name label still intact, are prized possessions of at least one or two *baratis* in the group. From behind their cover, these young men are able to ogle at the women to their heart's content, without inviting the ire of the elders.

But *baratis* are known for their nuisance value too. Getting drunk and complaining about the food and other arrangements are typical characteristics of *baratis*. Some even go to the extent of commenting adversely and provocatively at the dowry offered.

Many *baratis* carry guns or revolvers with them, just to impress the *beti-walas*. This had its uses about half-a-century ago, because the *baratis* had often to travel for days in bullock-carts to get to the bride's house, but these days carrying guns has become a status symbol.

In older times, a *barati* was presented a glass of copper or silver (depending on the bride's father's financial status), with some cash as a mark of *maan*. The bride-groom's father may or may not get any dowry, but the *baratis* only recognition is his *maan*, even till today.

Be he a child or an old man, all look forward to joining a *barat*. It has been seen on many an occasion that the old people are more keen on joining a *barat* than the younger ones. As also said elsewhere in this book, there is a joke relating to this keenness. An old man asked the bride-groom's father, who all were invited to join the *barat*. The father named some persons but not the old man, who asked him, *"Who else?"* The father named some more persons, again missing the old man. *"But this is a very small barat, who are still others?"* he asked again. At this, the father named him, *"And Tau, you too should be joining."* *"That is enough, more then enough. After all what is the use of collecting an Army of baratis,"* replied the old man.

HERE COMES THE *BATEU*

The son-in-law has his credence acknowledged universally, but in Haryana his status is doubly recognised in the sense that any guest in the countryside of this region is also called by the same name, *"bateu"*. For certain typicalities, the *bateu* has earned a niche in Haryanvi culture. A close study of his behaviour, dress, movement and nature, makes interesting revelations about this character.

The entire facade of the *bateu's* countenance is so self-speaking that you can identify him anywhere. He may visit any place attired in his daily routine wear, but when he has to oblige his in-laws by visiting them, he needs at least two-to-three days preparations. Once on his mission, he makes his presence felt in buses or trains, in the barber's shop and at tea stalls, or on the pavement, or while negotiating the payment he will offer to the cobbler for getting burnished his footwear.

It is a tradition in Haryana that when a *bateu* visits his in-laws' village for the first time after marriage, the village women throw coloured water on him. So conscious is he of his attire, that one may often come across a *bateu* changing his clothes under a tree some distance outside the village of the in-laws, so as to have his ironed clothes creased still. Oil trickles down his well lubricated side locks, giving off an aroma that makes it easy to trace his route.

The *bateu*, having had a shave at the bus stand, often reaches his in-laws' village with hair whitened at the back by some cheap powder applied by the barber. If his spouse is travelling with him, the responsibility of carrying the luggage (or even the baby, if they have one) rests on the shoulders of his better-half.

Bateu's lodging arrangements are made in the village *chaupal*. Howsoever talkative or an extrovert-type, he turns a very reserved person in his in-laws' village.

On reaching the *chaupal*, the *bateu* keeps standing till a bedsheet-on rare occasions a clean one, is spread on the cot. It is customary for him to hand-over is *lathi* to his brother-in-law at this stage. Conservative old women would never allow their sons to marry a brotherless spouse, for who will *"take-over the lathi from him?"*. When the *bateu* goes for an evening walk, the brother-in-law walks some feet ahead of him with the *lathi*.

There was a time when *bura* and *desi ghee* formed an important ingredient of a bateu's meals. Without it, the hospitality was incomplete. These days liquor, preferably country-made, must be offered to the *bateu* if he is to be kept in good humour.

After meals, a *lota* of milk from every, nearest relation, is sent for him as a symbol of respect. As his wife is considered to be the daughter of the entire village, he has the acquired right to be everybody's *bateu* in the entire village.

At the point of leaving, a *bateu* may drop his reserve and have some fun with his sisters-in-law.

CHHOOMANTAR

India is the land of *sadhus, mahatamas,* ascetics, or, so to say, godmen. They are men who possess some spiritual powers and most of them have renounced the world. Some live in *ashrams,* others go for meditation to the Himalayas, and some have their disciples scattered all over the place.

There is yet another class of these spiritual beings, which wanders from place to place and has no definite habitation, or even destination. They survive on the alms they get from devotees, sleep wnerever they find place, and are vagrants who travel mostly on foot.

In Haryana this class is known as *modas.* The word in local dialect, has the connotation of a man who is not a *grahasthi* or householder, who has renounced the world and freed himself of all responsibilities.

He is the most carefree and easy-go-lucky type of a wanderer. He has no family, no wealth, no ties, no reservations, no inhibitions. Indeed he is considered to be someone who is good for nothing and is easily dispensable. When old people are neglected by the family, they often complain that they have become redundant and are leading the life of a *moda.*

A *moda* is easily spotted. He has a coiled pyramid of hair on his head and a prolific-beard. He wears large, weighty earrings, a number of rosaries of *rudraksha or motis* around his

neck, arms and legs. He wears many *tabeezes* (metal covers tied with thread, said to have healing properties) around his neck, arms, or even the belly. On his forehead, or even chest, he wears ash.

Most of the *modas'* wear a *langoti* (a small piece of cloth to cover the genitals) and a *loi* to wrap their body. But there are others who sport loose saffron cassocks. Of course, this depends on the *moda's* choice—if he prefers to wear something.

Since basically a *moda* is a wanderer, he carries with him a *Kammandal* (an alms container), *jholi* for collecting wheat-flour which is offered to him, a blanket, a mat, a long *chimta* as a walking aid and also for protection. He also carries with him a T shaped wooden structure to rest his hand while counting the beads of the rosary while in deep concentration.

The *modas'* have all the semblance of other spiritual beings, but are considered by the village folk only as men-in-line for the spiritual destination. They are seldom taken to be real *sadhus*.

A *moda's* abode is either some abandoned *dharamshala*, or an inn, or even the village temple. He can be seen while on his mission, collecting alms, surrounded by village urchins. At each door step, he calls out: *"Alakh Niranjan"*, meaning thereby that some divine power has come at the door of the householder and the latter should show him his obeisance. The *moda* might also say: *"Jo dey uska bhala, jo na de uska bhi bhala* (Blessed be he who do donates, and he too who does not)."

Often, when the *moda* chants *"Alakh Niranjan"*, to complete the rhyme, the village urchins add, *"Age gaddi pichhe injan"*.

Sometimes, the *moda* prefers to sit in a meditating pose to attract the attention of passers-by who would propagate in the village that here is someone who is doing *tap* (meditation) for the well-being of the inhabitants of the village.

The women then start frequenting the site, and God-fearing villagers follow. They gather around the *moda* and bow before him, sit by his side with folded hands in an endeavour not to disturb his *tap*. Realizing perhaps that now there is a pretty good assembly of devotees, the *moda* opens his eyes, says *"Narain-Narain"* and exchanges glances with the people, making believe as if he has just "broken" his communion with the Supreme Being.

While all those who have gathered there would address the *moda* as *"baba ji", or "baba",* he would call them *"bacha"* (child), for a disciple is as fresh in the spiritual arena as is a child in the world.

Although, the rural women are easily fooled, men mostly detest the *moda* and are suspicious of him. Stories are rife of *modas* having been found in compromising positions with village women. A great hue and cry follows, culminating in the chasing of the *moda* out of the village.

Often, *modas* predict the lucky number for *satta* (gambling), and some are nearly drug addicts or criminals trying to escape the law.

But this is not to suggest that all *modas* are such persons. Most of these are indeed harmless and interested only in living by begging and wandering from place to place.

Though *modas* are mostly bachelors, there are instances of some finally getting married, having children, and turning house-holders.

Rural people try not to annoy the *modas* for fear of being cursed. Even bus conductors do not ask for fare from the *modas*. While traveling in a bus a *moda* might invite passengers to engage in spiritual conversation. And if some half-a-dozen passengers give a patient hearing to his discourses, he feels elevated. At this juncture, he may exploit the people's sentiments and ask for donation for begging is the first thing in his mind.

Modas' are rarely astrologers or palmists, though they are very good face-readers. They can judge whether or not a person is prone to be won over. And working on his reading of a person, a *moda* **goes on to tackle his victim accordingly.**

THE FORGOTTEN WISE MAN

Almost forgotten, *Boojh-Bujhakkar* has become a cliche. This expression had never been a part of any language, save the colloquial dialects. *Boojh-Bujhakkar* was in currency some four decades back in Haryana and its adjoining areas. The persons, who at a time claimed or deserved this appellation are still found in the region and are referred to or addressed as *Bara*, or *Bari*, in the case of a female. These words are self-explanatory and are indicative of the status accorded to his rank in the social hierarchy, even today.

Boojh-Bujhakkar's knowledge-bank was rife with solutions to the problems of the villagers, be they social religious, ritualistic, behavioural and even economic. And for this reason, coupled with the experience of *Boojh-Bujhakkar*, substantiated by his ripe age, the villagers approached him for this problem or that.

The *bara* or *bari* remembered the festival dates, religious occasions e.g. *Amavasya, Purnima, Silhi-Satam, Teej, Salooman, Karvachoth, Hoi, Bhaia Dooj, Kanagat* (Sharadh) etc. etc. Village ladies would approach the *bari* for knowing the procedures and rituals and other dogmatic ceremonies to be performed for a particular occasion. She would know the formalities of birth, mourning, marriages and worshipping the local *devies* and *matas* (Goddesses) and the

Dadda Khera. Dadda Khera is symbolic of the *pitras'* (ancestors) blessings with regard to the flourishing village, particularly the prolific progeny's prosperity.

On *Makra Sakranti*—a festival which coincides with the well-known *lohri,* the *bari's* 'standing order' was that everybody would take a bath before *kaleva* (breakfast). This was perhaps due to the villagers having a tendency not to take a bath and remain untidy, *"You will otherwise became a donkey in the next birth", the bari* would warn. If somebody had died in the *rishte-dari* (relatives) the *bari's* instructions to the mourners were, *"Reach the home of the deceased straight, and not any body else's on the way, for it will bring calamity on him".* This mourning is called *Nakharjana or Goda-nivana.*

People would approach the *bari* for interpretation of their dreams. If somebody's near and dear one had died in his dream, the *bari* would console the dreamer saying that he (the dead in the dream) would live for longer period and it was a good omen. If somebody had seen coins, snake, house wall or roof, damaged; it was declared as very bad and ominous. If some dead person had appeared in somebody's dream, the latter was advised to make donations to the poor or the brahmins.

For the *Boojh-Bujhakkar's* ever-readiness to oblige and find solution for every problem, he got no remuneration, either in cash or in kind. Unlike the village *purohit,* he would accept no donations but only *maan* or the recognition. He or she would however accept a *pagri, kurta, dhoti or a lotta* and *teel* etc. as a token of respect. No body would dare to make fun in the presence of the *bara or bari.* However for the *bari,* a pinch of *naswar* (snuff) or a puff of *Kali* (small hookah) were welcome things. Caste was no bar on assessing *Boojh-Bujhakkar's* status.

If you ask the *Boojh-Bujhakkar* about his age which confirms his being experienced, wordly-wise and the one who has seen the life from close quarters, he would not tell it to be less than eighty at least. In his own style he would tell that he was "six and eighty" meaning thereby, "eighty-six". He would say in a round-about manner that, *"that huge bar* (banyan tree) is of my *haan* (contemporary). Or he would say that he was born during the *kaal* (big famine) that befell the region about a century back. He would also tell that he had witnessed the *maar-kaat* (violence during partition), and that he had survived the *katak-wali* (epidemic that broke-out in 1930's) and also that he had seen *daka* (dacoity) at such and such *sahukar's haveli* with his own eyes. He would also talk about the *bundobust* (consolidation of land), and if one insisted too much, he could also predict the *parlow* (doom).

For the above described reasons, it is a strong belief still prevalent in the countryside that on the *Boojh- Bujhakkar's* death, if the children are made to walk under his or her *arthi* in the funeral procession; this added years to their lives.

For matrimonial consultations, the *Boojh-Bujhakkar* is still considered to be a marriage-bureau. He is well-informed about the good or bad *khandans* (clans). He knows how to match the statuses of different families. He is a past-master in balancing the matches. He knows the particular traits of different castes. He also knows the typicalities of different gotras or sub-castes.

He has fixed notions about suggesting the areas for matrimonial alliances. For example, he would disallow marrying one's daughter in *suba* (Union Territory of Delhi) for *suba-wala's* will put the girl on some *naukri* (Job). For a boy he would recommend Sirsa and its adjoining areas in Rajasthan and Punjab for *"they offer good dowry"*. *"Girls from Rohtak and Sonipat Districts are very clever and would disintegrate the joint family",* he warns.

He is very conservative with regard to inter-caste marriages and would not approve of them. He is known for looking down-upon a widow and an issue-less woman, or an only female children bearing lady, or a *bahu* (bride) having no brother. He is against female education. If some one marries out of his caste, *Boojh-Bujhakkar* is the one to order his *"Hookah-Pani-Band"* (get him socially ostracised). However, he is in favour of widow re-marriage but with restriction that it should be strictly endogamous.

Boojh-Bujhakkar, from his experience, and from the folktales, draws inferences which he co-relates with the daily happenings of the villagers. When it is the onset of winter, and he sees wasps flying and deserting their hives, he would declare that it was time for sowing wheat. Peacock's crowing is indicative of rains, he would tell. Howling dogs and mewing cats in a coarse voice at the dead of the night is declared as the sign of some catastrophe that is going to befall either the entire village or some family, according to the *Boojh-Bujhakkar.* He is a little too superstitious and is the one who allows the superstitions to gain ground with his own stamp of recognition and belief. The sight of a *kotri* or an owl is declared as ominous for the seer, where as the sight of *Son-chirya* makes the lady-luck smile at the seer and brings fortune to him; believes the *Boojh-Bujhakkar.*

He is known for quoting popular sayings to suit the occasion:

Barase Holi-Diwali

Isa ye Thoth, Isa ye Hali

(If it rains on Holi or Diwali, it makes no difference to the idler and hard-worker, for the land will automatically be soft for sowing).

The status of *Boojh-Bujhakkar* is quite sought after. And there are self-appointed or pseudo *Boojh- Bujhakkars* also. Once the goat of a shepherd, in an endeavour to eat the contents, put its mouth in a *baroli* (a small pitcher). She buried her neck too deep, that it did not come out of the *baroli*. Seeing this, the shepherd tried his best but could not succeed in releasing the animal's neck.

A neighbourer advised him to approach the *Boojh-Bujhakkar*. Seeing the pitiable condition of the goat, our friend the self-styled *Boojh-Bujhakkar* immediately sent for a sword. He ordered the shepherd to cut the neck of the goat. This done, he asked to break the *baroli* with a stone. *"And lo! the neck of the goat has been freed,"* the Boojh-Bujhakkar **declared and the gathering clapped.**

ENTER THE SYANA-EXIT ALL

"Well you have come either for a son; or for your cattle's recovery from illness; or to know as to who has stolen your ornaments; or whether you would win the litigation; or you will get a job; or after all who is after you for all your failures; or what should be the way out to damage your opponent's prospects in his new venture; or what stone is a favourable one for you; or what *tabeez* would make you perfectly healthy and strong; or.....!", and the list of the queries of a *syana*, or the exorcist, is as tell as his claims. By putting such queries to his clients, the *syana* would thus try to win their confidence and make them believe his occult powers and efficacy of the art of black-magic, which he claims to have mastered.

Syanas are not found in all the villages of Haryana but they are scattered throughout the region and each one has his own area of influence. Their clientele is also scattered extending to neighbouring states too. People in the countryside do not report theft to the police (for after all they are not *syanas*) but they rush to a particular place how-so-ever far off it is, to know about the thief from a *syana*.

This knowing-business is called *boojha*. When they approach the *syana* for a *bhoojha*, one or two of the above listed queries is put to them by the *syana*, and if by chance, or by the power a *syana* claims to possess, as the seekers believe, that particular query is relevant, the clients have already confirmed their faith in him.

A *syana* is normally addressed as *dada* or *dadi* in case she is a female. The fair-sex too practises black magic at many places. The *syana* is traditionally a round faced, dark-complexioned, bulging- round-eyed person with horizontally flourishing moustache almost reaching his temples. His agile tounge-movements visible through the toothless openings of his jaws, make him look a man really capable of driving out the evil spirits. He can be seen scratching, with his ugly long-nailed fingers his protruding dark-belly, on which sweat-drops trickle down.

Paradoxically, his female counterpart is a frail and bent lady with a wrinkled forehead and sunken cheeks. Her white hair and white horse-like teeth add fury to her facade. While in deep concentration, the *syana* would smoke his *chillum* excessively. The *syani* most of the times smokes a *biri*. And it is only after a strong-puff that they would divulge a name, a therapy or a *jugaar*.

The *syana's* paraphernalia include an empty gunny-bag to be used as a mat, a human skull, a broom, sarson-oil, a *chimta* (tong) a magic-vand, iron-rings, *tabeez*, some very common and cheap stones, branches of *neem* tree, an ash container and a whip to lash out the 'arrogant ghost', if the patient harbours one.

Quite contrary to an astrologer's predictions, prophecies and fore-telling, the *syana* mostly practises 'after telling'. He is the one who practises *"who could have done it"*. Very seldom he gives a concrete information otherwise he would only make generalized revelations. For example: *"Your thief lives within your house"*: or the stolen, article has been dumped in some well *"east of the village"*, or, *"his name begins with letter R or S....*and so on.

The *syana* is said to be possessing some heeling powers too. He will do a *Jhara* (some sort of a bloodless surgery) by making some odd, hand movements over the effected part of the body, he would prepare a *tabeez* for a particular disease and would prescribe tying it on the arms or legs, or wearing it as a rosari with a red or black thread. *"Don't burn or throw it"*, he would warn *"or else you are doomed and I too will be punished by the Kaal-Maharaj"*. Surprisingly, most of the *syanas* who practise black-magic die an unnatural and awesome death. The villagers ascribe this reason to the *syana's* having mis-used the *ridhi-sidhis* (magical powers recognised by Hindu mythology) for his personal, worldly gains.

Mostly, innocent and ignorant (some times even educated) village ladies constitute the clientele of the *syana*. These *syana*-seekers have blind faith in him. An infertile or frigid or issue-less female can do anything at the *syana's* bidding, if she is assured about her *maanta* (a prayer rewarded).

Stories are prevalent in the countryside where females kill some body else's children, drink their blood and hope to be blessed with a child at the *syana's* prescription. They are ready to walk stark-naked in the burial ground with a *dia* in their hands at the dead of night, if the *syana* recommends it as something which would invoke and please the *Kaal-Maharaj*, who would shower his blessings. But mostly these things end-up in scandals when the *syana*, taking advantage of the loneliness of the lady, seclusion of the burial place and "indication" of the *dia*, forces an outrageous, sexual attempt on his subject, the poor lady.

However, sometimes, his treating tricks have a psychological effect on the patients suffering from hysteria, depression hallucinations, and other problems as related to psychiatry. But the *syanas* are believed to be capable of healing cases where even pathology has developed and surgery is needed. This however can not be explained.

While performing these magical tricks the *syana* makes some unusual gestures like (as if) staring deep inside the earth, talking to himself, opening and closing the eyes in strange fashion, touching his ears as if repenting, spreading his fingers at something as if pulling something out, uttering irrelevant things, sprinkling water on the patient's face, throwing ash on the patient and dusting it with *neem* branches, chanting unintelligible *mantras* (hymns) all the time.

The *syana* does not necessarily inherit his powers from his ancestors rather he in a clandestine manner learns them from his unknown master. He sometimes prescribes donations to the Brahmins which would "reach" the client's *pitras* (dead-ancestors), he claims.

PLAY-FUL PRANKS OF A *NAAI*

"Beware of *navva (naai)* and *kavva* (crow)" is a famous saying in Haryana: for both the species are considered to be very intelligent; *naai*, although an illiterate fellow, is considered to be an experienced man. He is known for knowledge of scriptures, epics, folk-tales, folklores etc.

A *daroga ji* (police officer) was travelling in his jeep and ahead of him was walking a *naai* with his luggage on his head. The *daroga* sounded the horn, but the *naai* did not move aside. Annoyed at this, the *daroga* alighted from his jeep and gave a pretty good beating to the *naai* for having obstructed his way.

When the *daroga* came near his jeep and seated himself comfortably, then the *naai* approached him and asked in all innocence, *"Did you have some other job also or you just travelled a long distance to beat me up, Sahib"*.

Naai is the wittiest person in the village. His humour is not the rustic-humour rather it is safely padded under soft but sharp wit and sometimes, satire.

The *naai* plays a very important role in so far as keeping the different social groups knit-together is concerned. He will not divulge any body's secrets although he may be in the knowledge of so many. He would rather effect a compromise in different groups by his appeal and manipulative skills. If the *naai* knows that there is rivalry between two persons, he would

never exploit it rather he would most of the times, be a mediator and will unite people, for every body has faith in him.

Although, the *naai* may fish-out the secrets while shaving somebody's chin but he will never divulge those to anybody else. He is very much the 'man who keeps secrets'.

In the rural cultural milieu, if a girl doesn't find a good in-laws house, she curses her *naais*, (and brahmins too). *Naai* too was sometimes back a marriage information bureau. He knew which family would match the financial, social and other statuses of another family. And keeping this in mind, and from his record, the *naai* would suggest a boy or a girl, on demand.

Naai is still said to be responsible for many arrangements during the marriage ceremony. He is the one who invites everyone on the host's behalf. He is the one who serves as a link between the bride and the bride-groom's sides, for resolving any sort of crisis, that may emerge.

If the lunch is delayed and the entire *barat* is looking for the *naai* to turn-up, he would make his importance felt and would assume airs of an informer about the readiness or otherwise of lunch. In marriages, *naai* is the make-up man for the bride-groom, and his female counterpart, the *naain*, is the make-up woman for the bride.

Naai has to deal with different strata of the rural society and in his public-dealing he doesn't allow his own identity to be shadowed by anybody else. He is a known psychologist. He is a different man with youngesters still different with the old people, and quite different with the children. Even the village urchins are his best friends. He is a known face-reader. All this is ascribed, perhaps to his experience and his travelling.

Naai is not at all a harmful person rather, with his tacts he can win many a heart. Although he is a first rate chaunist but his sycophancy is recognised and even the most simple ruralite knows the *naai's* nature. Thus, he is a creature who offends none and pleases all.

Sometimes the *naai* indulges in rumour mongering also but he means no harm to anybody by doing so. The *naai* is very quick in giving answers. There is a saying prevalent in the countryside: *"O Naai how long is my hair?"* asks the customer. *"Very, soon you will see it, (cut) before your eyes, dear,"* replies the *naai*.

Once at a marriage function, some friends of a *naai* challenged him if he could use his tricks and arrange stomach-fuls of milk for them. *"O, yes!"* said the *naai* and shouted, *"Look-out! Beware! the dogs have spoilt the whole milk in the containers"*. The master of the house on hearing this ordered that the milk should not be used. And then the *naai* pleaded, *"Sarkar, in that case why can't we ask these good-for-nothing fellows (his friends) to drink this milk. Such spoilt milk does no harm to them"*. **And Lo! the *naai* arranged milk for everybody.**

MISCHIEF AND INNOCENCE PUT TOGETHER

Pali is the name given to a shepherd in Haryana. Although he is known, for his innocence, meekness, submissiveness and gentleness of temperament, universally. These traits of character are in-born in the *pali* but he develops them by slow degrees, chiselled by the environment he has to live in; at the same time he is also one of the most mischievious of other characters found in Haryanvi rural society.

When a male fathers many sons, in the rural setting of this region, he is proud of them all but not the one who is to hold charge of rearing the cattle and looking after them. So the *pali* is the discarded one amongst the sons in the family. He has seldom had his schooling, that too not beyond second or third standard, of our rating the school education. The only redeeming feature for the *pali* here is, that he is not bothered about education for the fear of the school teacher's batons and never complains to anybody about the step-motherly treatment meted out to him, not only by his family members but the society at large.

Pali's only job is to look after the cattle, sheep goats etc. when they roam about in the pastures for grazing. Thus he collects them at an appointed place at the village and takes them to the jungle. He also takes the entire herd to some place where water is available, once or twice a day; and in the evening hands them over to their respective masters or owners.

Pali too has his typical past time and rustic habits. His sports include jumping from a tree, or in water. He would throw some metallic object on the live electricity wires and would watch the sparks. While conversing normally, he may act swiftly and stretch his hand beyond a certain height making some old punk's spectacles fly off in the air. He may be patting some body's waist for no reason, or thumping someone's thighs, or do clapping coupled with wild laughter, or even indulge in hugging and hanging by someone and pulling him down, out of ecstasy. He eats a little too much, for he seldom has a ready meal. For these reasons put together the *pali* is an ostracised being.

Mischief and *Pali* are synonymous with each other. From a *pali*, there is always, *"only he and none else would have done it,"* sort of expectation, where some mischief is involved. He would climb some tree, eat the fruit and throw the seeds on some passer-by, at the same time hiding himself in the leaves. At times, when a train is moving he would make faces at the passengers; show them his thumb (a symbol of do-what-ever-you can); bare himself, not out of an exhibitionist's pleasure but for the confirmation that after all the train is not going to stop for his petty 'offence'. To travellers, he would always tell a wrong direction, if he is asked about the location of a particular village or place.

Pali is always a very good swimmer. He is very quick at killing snakes or any wild, small animals. At the request of the village old ladies, he fetches them wild-growths, herbs, roots etc. of medicinal value. He is a record-keeper of cattle health. He would tell the date of a particular animal's impregnation; and also if some cow or buffalo is having her oestrus period and he 'arranges' for their mating also.

Pali is the propagator of the super-natural too. In hot summer afternoons, when there is no body around, except the kites soaring the sky, he would run towards the village and tell horror-stories to the villagers; that he saw a man in all white, and the man transformed himself into a bullock and then a dog and then a pig and then a cat and then he vanished. And he saw smoke rising from that place thereafter. It is only out of this instinct that he *"cries-wolf"*.

Pali's paraphernalia include a *lathi*, a water container of dried up bottle-gourd, a cow dung cake, a small *chillum*, a pinch of snuff and that of tobacco, a small piece of cloth to cover his head and very rarely a pair of *jutis*.

A transistor has taken place of his conventional flute, for entertainment. But the agony is that the *pali* does not know which station he has tuned on. Be it, *"a ting-tong of Vivid Bharti"* or *"This is the eastern service of BBC; our next programme will be Sanskrit,"* pali **gives them all a patient hearing.**

THE ENVIABLE PHOJI

Since ages, people of Haryana and the adjoining areas are well-known for being warriors par excellence. Although their fighting tactics have not been recognised by the historians as those of Shiva ji; e.g. his Guerilla war-fare. Of course, our tactics is often dubbed as *"Maar Kai bhagjya or khaa kei soja"* (Escape after beating, and sleep after eating).

But the Haryanvi soldiers are known for giving a tough fight to the enemy. While fighting out anything, the Haryanavi soldiers care the least for any consequences and for this reason even the Britishers and the Mughals had 'used' these very people to check their enemies even in alien lands.

The warriors and soldiers, who are now on the right side of seventy or eighty claim to have fought bravely against the enemies of the British empire. For the Britishers, these warriors fought in countries like Germany, Italy, Turkey and Egypt etc. and sustained injuries; died in the battle field and some of them even earned a niche in the temple of warriorship and were credited with having won awards of those times.

Since these warriors had been associated with the English people, they still have the hangover of the English officers' style of walking and talking and for that matter most of the Army officers still imitate the English. The soldiers who are mostly from lower ranks are known as *phojis* and those from the higher ranks as *sahibs* in Haryana's rural setting.

When the *phoji* reaches his native place, he assumes the same english postures of walking and talking for the reason described above. When any reference is made to their ownself, regarding their own deeds and experience of army-life, they will initiate the conversation with the phrase *hum-log*. To the kith and kin of the *phojis* and the other ruralities, they try to give an impression that while being in the Army they have been 're-christened' as a different category people than their own; and a derogatory term 'bloo....civilians' is also a coinage in the Army-slang.

Phoji is known for using broken english in the presence of simple, rural-folk who may not understand what they mean, and thereby, giving an impression to the people around that "Our *phoji* is not less than an English speaking Commissioned officer of the Army". The innocent villagers would thus feel happy over the elevation and the *phoren* style of conversation. All shades of jokes are prevalent in the country side about the *phoji's* conversation and other routine sort of things.

Once while sitting with his mother, sister and *bhabi*, a *phoji* was narrating his experiences in the army. The *bhabi* was in an advanced stage of pregnancy and curiously asked her *devar*, the *phoji*, as to what was his routine in the army. To this he replied, that he began his day with drill. The poor wenches could not understand what 'drill' was, and asked the *phoji* to explain to them clearly, what did he begin his day with. The *phoji* said, *"To make you understand, I will be giving a 'demo'* (demonstration), *come on stand in a line!"* All the three ladies did what the *phoji* wanted them to do.

Thus commanded our friend, the *phoji*, *"Saamne dekho,* (look forward), *harkat nahin* (no movements)," and pointing towards his pregnant *bhabi* he said *"Aye Jawan, pet under aur chhati bahar* (squeeze your protruding belly inside and make your breasts bulge out)". All the three ladies pushed the *phoji* out of the house, who had in all innocence, 'demonstrated' to bring home the point 'drill' to his female family members.

Once a *phoji* who was posted in some very cold region, wrote to his father that he needed his family there, and the father should send the family immediately. The wife is often referred to as family by the *phojis*. Failing to understand, what a family was, and realizing that the son is posted in a very high colder region, so he must have needed his *razai* (quilt), the father sent the same to his son. At this the *phoji* remarked in all desperation *"you gaamris (villagers) will remain gaamris, even if your son becomes a General in the Army."*

A *phoji* reached his village with a fellow soldier. He told his mother that food is to be prepared for him and his lance-naik. Having prepared the food, the mother told his son that his food had been served in the kitchen and that (fodder) of his lance-naik was served in the stable. *Phoji* objected to it and told the mother that his lance-naik would eat with him only. Bewildered, the mother said, *"But how are you going to have your food with a horse."* The innocent mother thought lance-naik was the horse who had come with her son.

Ghee-bura is served in the rural areas when some guest happens to visit some body's place, as recognition of his status of a guest or *bateu*. While serving food to his son, the *phoji*, his old mother having put a heap of *bura* in his *thali*; she started adding *desi ghee* to the *bura*. When the *phoji* saw that his mother had put a little more *ghee*, he shouted *"Halt."* Disturbed at this, the poor mother put the entire container full of *ghee* in the *thali* and started looking at his guest-like son in astonishment. Thus snubbed the *phoji* his mother, *"Old lady,*

the entire squad stops at the command 'Halt' and you could not control your ghee container". Mothers would be mothers afterall!

As already said the *phoji* speaks broken English while in the presence of not only his colleagues but his relatives in the village, as well. Two *phojis* were passing through a street in the village and seeing a bitch sleeping on their way, one of them remarked *"See friend the dogni (bitch) is sleeping"*. Added his fellow *phoji* *"Sleepan de, sleepan de iske din hein"* (let her sleep, she too has her days). Perhaps the *phoji* wanted to convey that every dog has his day.

Once a *phoji's* friend asked him as to how was shooting taught to them. The *phoji* immediately took in his hands, the nearest *lathi*; took the lying position and started aiming at someone. At this juncture the poor friend happened to cross on to the other side of the *phoji*, in front of his *lathi's* 'firing range'. Thus cried our friend the *phoji* *"You idiot, you are in the firing range, but it is none of your fault, I have myself forgotten to make some-body stand up with a red warning flag, or else you would have been killed.*

The *phoji* is known for telling his 'ever waiting wife' that he would take his "dinner in the afternoon" and "lunch in the evening".

After retirement, the *phoji* settled in the village is supposed to be a strict disciplinarian. He can be often seen teaching discipline to the simple, rural-folk who do not seem to be knowing any restrictions imposed on them in the garb of discipline. But the *phoji's* status is recognised and he is a person who is known to be above-board; has been in the service of the nation, and is known to be quite fair in his dealings. Even in the ruralities' assembly or the Panchayat, the *phoji's* word carries weight with the members, because he is always considered to be a neutral mediator.

All that a *phoji* is liked by his friends in the village is also a bottle of Rum or an abandoned uniform.

By adding fiction to the facts, most of the times, the *phoji* is known for impressing the gathering around him while relating his experiences in the Army, in the battle field or in some alien-land. Some times his boasting and other tales make him really appear a man who is brave, challenging type, and bold in the natives' eyes, and this is true to a larger extent.

At the fag end of the *phoji* episode, I would like to relate another example of *phoji's* broken English. While in his village a *phoji* asked his wife to handover his *lungi* to him. As it was a habit with him to ask for the *lungi*, after taking a bath, from his fellow soldiers in the Unit; he asked his wife to fetch him the same *lungi*. The poor Haryanvi lady could not understand what a *lungi* was and asked her husband to explain to her clearly, in Haryanvi and not in *'angrezi'*, what he exactly wanted. Realising the 'poor knowledge of English' of his wife, he said *"Bhagwaan' (darling) please handover my half-dhoti to me"*. **The wife was naturally proud of her 'English-speaking Husband.'**

EVIL-DOING AT ITS HEIGHT

Narad is quite famous for his trickeries in the Hindu Mythology. *Kuparia* of Haryana fame epitomizes *Narad*, so far as poking one's nose in every body else's affairs is concerned. Although, *Kuparia* and his likes are found in every society, but this land's *Kuparias* have certain typicalities found clung to their person. In plain English, we can call *Kuparia* a man capable of doing everything that is not smooth and straight; or an evil-doer who will not desist from going to any extent, even if some harm is meant to any-body, irrespective of any considerations, even without bothering for the consequences.

Kadhi-bigar (one who spoils the soup) can be another epithet given to *kuparia*. There is a famous saying in Haryana that if some matrimonial alliance breaks down due to the mischief played by some one, it is none other than our friend, Mr. *Kadhi-bigar*.

Once when the talks of engagement of a boy and a girl were in progress, the *kuparia* got the news. He immediately suspended his mission and approached the scene. He stood at the door of the girl's father and cried at him at a loud pitch telling him that the *patwari*, (revenue clerk) had come to the village *chaupal*, and that he wanted to speak to him. At this the girl's father, recognising *kuparia's* voice, told him to inform the *patwari* that he would be coming soon. But the *kuparia*

insisted again at the same pitch of voice, that the *patwari* wanted to see him immediately.

The girl's father sensing the evil designs of *kuparia* replied in a rather humble tone that he was busy with some very important job and that he would be seeing the *patwari* immediately after that. Thus, spoke our friend *kuparia*, *"All right dear, I can understand your problem, neither you have an inch of land nor do I, so patwari's call is immaterial for both of us,"* making it clearly audible to the girl's would be father-in-law and other guests, and indicating that the girl's father was a very poor man. Subsequently the engagement gave way, thanks to *kuparia's* 'intervention'.

Kuparia is a master at spreading rumours. His rumour mongering does have some sort of a significance because the *kuparia* is said to be a well-informed man, despite his bad reputation. If some one commits a mischief and the *kuparia* comes to know of it, you don't need another P.R. man to get the affair publicised.

Mischief mongering also has always been another past-time of *kuparia*. He would put water in the fresh *chillum* of the assembly of the spectacled old punks, who can not see beyond a certain distance. He would block their *hookah* pipes with a wooden straw. He would give wrong directions to the running water channels or make holes in them by using his *lathi* thereby watering the entire crop, that does not require much irrigation e.g. cotton, maize, barley etc.

He would chase the animals in some one's field and inform the owner that so and so's cattle were destroying his crops. A scuffle would definitely ensue but the *kuparia's* job is done.

Kuparia can not bear the sight of monkeys in the village. He would chase them out of the village; perhaps two like-minded animals can not put-up together in a small place, like a village. *Kuparia* is mad after the mad-dogs and would beat them to death or bury them alive or put them in a gunny bag, tie its head and throw it in the river or the village water pond. He would catch the wasps by their wings and tie a thread to their legs and enjoy their "slowed-motion-flight".

If some *Panchayat* is holding a session under some tree, the *kuparia* will never miss the chance and spare his *gulel* (a catapulting agent) and would make the. bee-hive on the branch of that tree, his target, thereby provoking the wasps to form a swarm above the *panchayat* members' heads, who would run helter-skelter. The session is thus adjourned sine-die. The members know it pretty well that it could be none else than the *kuparia*, who is behind the whole mischief. But even the Panchayats can not 'harm' a *kuparia* a well known shameless creature.

Kuparia will tell his cronies that if they are able to net a squirrel (a small tree climbing, bushy-tailed animal, with red or grey fur) and bury it half-a-foot deep in the ground, they will find a *chawani* (a four anna coin) at that place after a month of the 'burial'. This, the *kuparia* does to keep his cronies engaged in some mischief or the other, for the simple reason that a swift animal like a squirrel is hard to catch. No doubt, the *kuparia* is a master at killing snakes.

Election time is the mischief time for the *kuparia*. He would tear-off the party flag of the candidate or would puncture his vehicle's tyres or deflate them. If the canvassing party does not oblige him with demands of posters and flags etc. (of which he may understand nothing), he may even go to the extent of even pelting stones at the vehicles and breaking wind screens etc.

If the candidate is wise enough to cultivate the *kuparia* and offer him some money or to raise slogans in his favour, he can never be sure about it, for the *kuparia* and his cronies may indulge in raising slogans against the very candidate and run away from the scene shouting at the top of their voice *"Harega bhai harega, so and so, harega"*.

On certain festivals the *kuparia* is the master mind behind so many mischiefs. For example, on *Teej* when it is the swinging season, he may weaken the rope and enjoy the swingers dashing down, on the ground. On *Diwali* he can be seen stealing away the *diyas* (earthen-lamps) or the candles etc.

It is a common sight on the occasion of *Holi* to see *kuparia* being carried in a funeral procession by his fellow urchins. When the saner elements in the locality object to it and snub the processionists, the 'dead *kuparia*' becomes alive and jumps from the shoulders of the 'pal-bearers'. Of course he leaves the place but none can be sure that an infuriated *Kuparia* will not burn some-body's *Jhuggi* (hut). On this day he would go to the village cremation ground at the dead of the night and shout in a voice resembling that of a jackal, thereby, making the village children afraid of the ghost-like voices coming from the funeral place. But every-body else in the village knows that it is only the *Kuparia* who is at the back of whole affair.

His other mischiefs include appearing in the guise of a stranger before some lonely inhabitant of the village and embarrassing him to the extent that he has to seek the neighbourers' help to get rid of the *kuparia*.

He can be seen lying on the busy roads of the village in such a condition as would resemble the sight of a dead-body, lying in the dark, unattended. He would form a small court with the help of other village urchins and he himself posing a self-appointed judge can be seen passing judgements.

The punishments of these 'summary-trials' are interesting in themselves. Some of them being: asking the alleged accused to jump from a certain height; to touch the nearest bee-hive; to twist the tail of a ferocious dog; to remove the spectacles of a responsible villager; to catch by the horns an offensive, he-buffalo; to jump into some deep well; to break the street light bulbs etc. etc.

All said and done I will now come to the rescue of the *Kuparia* by quoting an example when a *Kuparia* saved a life and was thus redeemed in my eyes, at least.

I remember when a quack came to my village in the garb of a *babaji* or of a *moda*. He had it proclaimed in the village that he had permanent cures for diseases like hysteria, epilepsy etc. The quack was puffing up in an old, abandoned *dharamshala* (inn).

An innocent villager and his wife took their teenaged-girl to the quack. The latter prescribed rubbing ash on the breasts of the girl, in isolation. The poor parents allowed this treatment. Our friend *kuparia* came to know of it and climbed the three storied inn to see from one of the windows what the quack would do. The latter took the girl inside, stripped her of her clothes, gagged her mouth, and attempted rape on her.

Kuparia could not bear the sight. He raised a hue and cry and jumped from above on the quack. When the parents break-opened the door they found the *kuparia* murdered by the *moda* with his *chimta* (tong).

I remember the village wenches weeping like any thing on that day. **Really, it was the day of the *Kuparia*.**

NO CHAUNISM THIS, ATLEAST

Every society in India does have in it persons who are known extroverts, and humorists. They are professional composers who would say even the most unpalatable reality in lighter vein. They will often speak in a tongue-in-cheek manner and would evoke the 'desired effect'. They are known for their typical prose, blank-verse and rhythm styles so far as their 'creativity' is concerned. Their pun can have so many meanings ranging from dangerous and intolerable ones to highly accepted ones; of course, depending on their reception by their audience.

In Haryana, this class is known for being flippant singers of virtues and vices and are called *dooms*. These are *mirasis* by profession owing to their musical and poetic talents. They are also known as *bhands* for their humorous and clownish styles of behaviour.

Doom is very careful about his dress. He is always found wearing a (comparatively) neat and clean *kurta-dhoti*. This is perhaps because he is a well-travelled man and is a wanderer, and realizing that while visiting *pardes* (an alien land) he should make his presence felt by making people look at him and admire him for his 'sobriety'.

You must have heard of people singing in praise of God and the super-natural; but the *doom* sings in praise of his fellow human beings. In his social intercourse, he is a meek, almost lamb-like and an unharmful person, whose very sight is a

pleasant thing for the ruralities. This is because they always expect a *chambola* (a couplet); a *ragni* (folk-lore particular to Haryana); a *kissa* (an anecdote from legends); a *bhajan* (a song in praise of God from the epics or scriptures); a *taan* (a tune from his *saarangi* or *iktara*); and even a *lehra* (a melody from his been).

Any body who suffers any sort of gloom starts smiling if the doom is in sight for the latter will definitely lighten the burdensome gloom by his jubilant jokes pregnant with humour and wit. This was perhaps a reason which is ascribed to the 'now extinct' (but they are very much there) *zamindar's* or the landlord's hiring the regular services of a *doom* as their 'court-jester'.

A *doom* is a born-lover of music. Readers will be surprised to know that the *doom* with a little training at the hands of his master, mostly his father, learns very complicated *rags, taals, dhuns, sargams, saptaks* etc. etc. at a very quick speed. When his fingers fly on the gamuts, no body can doubt the inborn talents of a doom. As already said, *saarangi* and *iktara* are his favourite instruments.

His talents are also recognised by the *saangis* (a group of singers and actors who present cross-road concerts for the entertainment of villagers). When some *saang* is to be staged the *doom* assumes airs of an organiser and is given the duty of rotating the *hookah* amongst the stage performers. He is the one who encourages the *saangis* by giving due *daat* (appreciation) by associating the spectators with him. He speaks in a loud tone *"chala paat gaya bhaiyo* (brothern, it is a wonderful performance)", and *"rukka maach gaya rai* (the sangees have stolen the show, dears)".

Doom's status as an able Public Relations Man is recognised by all and sundry in the area. If he so wishes he can down-grade anybody for he is the person who travels a lot and people feel that their reputation, bad or good, travels with their *doom*. Thus the villagers give the *doom* his due, as remuneration for singing in their praise and publicise their *rutba* or influence. The *doom* collects these donations in the form of food-grains only at the time when the crops have matured. If a *doom* is denied donations, he can, in a silent manner of course, damage any body's reputation. So every body in the village keeps the *doom* in confidence and in good humour.

If a *doom* is asked to comment on something, he would do it in such a manner as would harm none. There is a saying prevalent in the countryside of Haryana that once *Laxmi* (Goddess of wealth) and *Tota* (misery personified) went to a *doom* and asked him to comment as to who of the two was superior to the other. The *doom* could not annoy any of the two for *Laxmi* would deprive him of his wealth, and *Tota* would shower miseries on him.

So, the *doom* thought of a clever plan and asked both of them to walk a certain distance ahead of him. Then he beckoned them to his side. Thus commented the *doom*, "look dears, watching your gait, I have to say that *Laxmi* is superior when she visits somebody and *Tota* is superior when he leaves". **And the *doom* saved his skin by pleasing both.**